Plone 3 for Education

Break the webmaster bottleneck by empowering instructors and staff

Erik Rose

PACKT PUBLISHING

BIRMINGHAM - MUMBAI

Plone 3 for Education

First published: January 2010

Production Reference: 2161209

Published by Packt Publishing Ltd.
32 Lincoln Road
Olton
Birmingham, B27 6PA, UK.

ISBN 978-1-847198-12-9

www.packtpub.com

Cover Image by Vinayak Chittar (vinayak.chittar@gmail.com)

Credits

Author
Erik Rose

Reviewers
Jordan Carswell
Steve McMahon
Denys Mishunov
Jeffrey G. Pittman

Acquisition Editor
Rashmi Phadnis

Development Editor
Dhiraj Chandiramani

Technical Editors
Mehul Shetty
Tarun Singh

Indexer
Hemangini Bari

Editorial Team Leader
Akshara Aware

Project Team Leader
Lata Basantani

Project Coordinator
Srimoyee Ghoshal

Proofreaders
Andie Scothern
Chris Smith

Graphics
Nilesh R. Mohite

Production Coordinator
Dolly Dasilva

Cover Work
Dolly Dasilva

About the Author

Erik Rose has consulted on the launch of dozens of education-domain Plone sites at Pennsylvania State University. As a lead developer at Penn State's WebLion group, he works with professors and departmental webmasters on everything from courseware sites to complex custom applications. Rose maintains several popular Plone plug-ins—including Faculty/Staff Directory, WebServerAuth, and CustomNav—and contributes to many other projects, including Archetypes, RedirectionTool, ArchGenXML, CSSManager, and Trac. He created WebLion Hosting, a large-scale Plone hosting platform, and founded the WebLion Wiki, now one of the largest repositories of Plone knowledge on the web.

Rose also takes an active role in Plone itself. He is a member of the Plone Foundation and serves on both the Plone 4 and Plone 5 framework teams, acting as spokesperson for the latter. He speaks at world and regional Plone conferences about software architecture, hosting, and documentation, and can be found helping people daily on the #plone IRC channel.

Thanks to Dr. Jeffrey Pittman for his revealing case study on teaching courses with Plone and for his countless edits; Jon Stahl and David Glick for some scintillating discussions about blogging; Denys Mishunov for taking the time to think deeply about Plone calendaring and for his many helpful edits; Steve McMahon for maintaining the excellent PloneFormGen product and for his razor-sharp suggestions; Joel Burton for his battle-tested usability tips and PloneFormGen recipes; Rob Porter for several enlightening theming chats; Malthe Borch for `z3c.jbot`, which made the *Styling Your Site* chapter much more accessible; Jordan Carswell for reading all my drafts and offering useful feedback; Craig Haynal for his Squid configuration work and for the "ZopeSkel is madlibs for Plone" metaphor; Martin Aspeli and Veda Williams for their practical book-writing advice; Buddy the Dog for coming to check on me during many late nights and offering his invaluable grammar tips; and most of all, my wonderful new wife Lauren for lending me to this project for a year.

About the Reviewers

Jordan Carswell has been a web developer in Higher Education for the past twelve years. He has used Plone to develop websites in a variety of contexts, from small grants to large institution-wide projects.

The reviewer would like to thank the Plone community for an open source project that has benefitted him and many other web developers around the world.

Steve McMahon lives in Davis, California, and works as a Plone consultant and integrator with Reid-McMahon, LLC, which specializes in working with non-profit organizations. He's currently secretary of the Plone Foundation, caretaker for PloneFormGen and is working on several new features for Plone 4.0.

Steve is one of the authors of Practical Plone, and was a technical reviewer for Plone 3 Theming.

Denys Mishunov is a Plone expert specializing in Plone themes development since early 2004. During his Plone career, he worked as a freelancer with many Plone consulting companies distributed all over the world and participated in a large number of Plone projects by providing services in design and Plone themes development. Denys is the Plone core contributor and author of some publicly available add-ons for Plone. Originally working as a freelancer in Ukraine, he has established one of the first Plone 3 projects in the world, Web Couturier, some days before the official release of Plone 3. The project doesn't exist in its original form anymore, but has provided some, previously commercial, packages as open source products for Plone Collective.

In 2008, Denys moved to Norway to work with one of the leading Plone consulting companies, Jarn (ex-Plone Solutions).

Denys was also a technical reviewer for the book *Plone 3 Theming* by Veda Williams.

Jeffrey G. Pittman, **Ph.D.**, is a geologist with an interest in paleontology, sedimentology and stratigraphy, and computer applications. He has studied dinosaur fossils and footprints in the South-Central and Western United States and in Mexico, emphasizing the Cretaceous Period. He has taught geology in college for over 20 years, most recently using Linux servers, Python, and Zope/Plone for content delivery, discussion, and student work.

For Lauren

Table of Contents

Preface

Why do so many schools have terrible websites? Talk to the people in charge, and you rarely find incompetence. On the contrary, the web team is often the first to express dissatisfaction, but their hands are tied by some combination of these problems:

- *The webmaster bottleneck.* Everyone is busy. If editing web content is any harder than clicking and typing, faculty and staff get discouraged, and the web team (or, heaven forbid, the solitary webmaster) ends up doing everything.
- *Web team overcommitment.* The people who handle the web are stretched too thin, also handling desktop support, server maintenance, or application development. This leaves little time for web work. Without sophisticated tools for site maintenance, any remaining time goes to drudge work on basic navigation and formatting.
- *Outgrown infrastructure.* A site of a dozen pages can comfortably be maintained with a copy of Dreamweaver and Apache. But sticking with the same tools as the site grows leads to a constant struggle to maintain consistent navigation, style, and structure.

These problems weigh on the web team, leading to overwork, poor or out-of-date content, and disorganized, inconsistent sites. But it doesn't have to be that way.

Though no software can magically transform bad sites into good, a good content management system such as Plone provides out-of-the-box navigation and formatting consistency. It gives your faculty and staff a simple visual editor so they can contribute just by clicking and typing. It even lets you enforce review procedures to make sure that content quality is up to snuff. In short, Plone lets the computers handle the repetitious work they are good at, freeing humans to make your site's content, structure, and visual design worthy of the organization it represents.

Why Plone for schools?

Plone is a great choice for educational institutions, from small local districts to large universities. There are high quality add-on products for faculty and staff directories, calendaring, form generation, audio and video, and more. Even better, its out-of-the-box features fit comfortably into the atmosphere of nontechnical faculty, tight budgets, and weird legacy requirements: Plone is...

- *Friendly to end users.* An instructor who knows Microsoft Word can be posting content in half an hour, safely constrained by your chosen set of styles so your site looks consistent.
- *Zero-integration.* Users need only a web browser, and it doesn't matter which one. Plone works with Internet Explorer, Safari, Firefox, screen readers, and anything else standards-compliant.
- *Cheap.* Plone is free to download and use, where comparable commercial systems can cost a large university hundreds of thousands of dollars per year in licenses and support.
- *Industrial-strength.* Plone supports workflow, fine-grained access control, change tracking, sophisticated search, metadata, and more. It has a wider scope than blog-derived projects like WordPress and more out-of-the-box functionality than frameworks like TurboGears.
- *Extensible.* Plone touts a pervasive plug-in architecture; hundreds of ready-made add-on products are free to download. Failing that, the Python language lends itself to dynamic patching, and, failing that, the whole stack is open-source, so you can modify it directly.
- *Scalable.* Configured as in the *Going Live* chapter, a single server can deliver hundreds of anonymous requests per second. If you reach the capacity of one machine or want to guarantee zero downtime, several can be clustered together.
- *Interoperable.* Plone integrates with academia's user management services like LDAP, Active Directory, Kerberos, CoSign, and more. It comes ready to talk to your existing applications through relational databases or via standards like XML-RPC and iCal.

Conquering complexity

With all of these goodies comes one notable challenge: internal complexity. While visitors and content contributors have nothing to worry about, your web team will find Plone, and the layers beneath, tricky to master from a development standpoint. The code may not be spaghetti, but it's at least an imposing plate of lasagna.

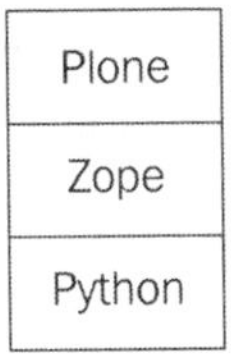

> Plone is content management functionality set atop the Zope framework, which serves HTTP and provides persistence, sessioning, authentication, authorization, transactions, templating, and other basic facilities. Both Plone and Zope are written in Python.

Most of this complexity is a side effect of maturity. Plone, itself five years old, is a largely user-interface layer atop the Zope framework, which has over a decade of experience tied up in its code. In that time, Zope and Plone have encountered and solved countless problems—problems you won't have to resolve in your site. However, the price of those solutions was change, and sometimes the old ways hung around long after the new ones arrived. As a result, it's not always clear which way of doing things is preferred. You can't always believe the comments in the code. And learning by example is dicey, because you never know when your example is based on obsolete practices.

That's where this book comes in.

I've been making mistakes in Plone for years—so you don't have to. This book filters through the legacy cruft so you know what to believe. It points you to the best add-on products by the most reputable authors. It highlights future-proof APIs and practices while steering clear of the volatile bleeding edge. Even if you are the only Plone person in your organization, you can start from a position of experience.

What this book covers

Each chapter will guide you through solving a common education-domain use case. Most chapters stand on their own so you can use this as a reference book without having to "eat the whole elephant." After all, if you're already suffering from webmaster bottleneck, you won't have time for very large bites between interruptions.

Chapter 1 - *Creating Courses*: Represent a bare-bones course in Plone, for optional embellishment in later chapters. Post syllabi, course materials, and due dates, and distribute assignments online. Collect feedback from students throughout the semester to drive continuous improvements.

Chapter 2 - *Calendaring*: Due dates, athletic schedules, concerts, lectures—track them all using Plone's built-in event support. Bring in the third-party Plone4Artists Calendar product to add wall-calendar-like views and support for repeating events, and explore some best-of-breed organizational schemes based on real-time filtering with collections.

Chapter 3 - *Showcase Personnel with Faculty/Staff Directory*: The Faculty/Staff Directory product is practically a departmental website in a box. Showcase your instructors, staff, and students; highlight their areas of expertise; and publish their biographies and contact details. Group people into committees and departments, and use those groupings for display and access control. Finally, get a sneak peek into the future of the Faculty/Staff Directory product, which I help develop.

Chapter 4 - *Extending Faculty/Staff Directory*: Faculty/Staff Directory does a lot, but every school has some custom requirements. Toward this, the product supports an extensibility framework for adding fields to its data types. In this chapter, take this framework for a test drive. Add fields to keep track of a fax number and a list of scholarly publications. Just as you need them, you'll find plenty of sidebars explaining portions of Plone infrastructure, from Archetypes to adapters.

Chapter 5 - *Blogs & Forums*: In a university, large class sizes limit class discussions and individual attention, while travel budgets limit the number of professional conferences where faculty can present. In this chapter, set up blogs and forums to counter both problems—giving students more class interaction and helping faculty build professional prominence. We'll find the best Plone blog products and explore practical suggestions of how to use blogs in the classroom. We'll also take the undisputedly top forum product for a spin and see how to use it to let students support each other, saving office hours and after-school help for those who need them most.

Chapter 6 - *Audio & Video*: Some instructors worry that publishing audio or video of lectures will hurt class attendance, but higher-ed institutions who have experimented with services like iTunes U have found just the opposite. In this chapter, learn how to publish audio and video in Plone and create podcasts so students can retrieve the latest materials automatically. Also learn how to bootstrap an iTunes U presence for your school, offering your materials on the iTunes Store and tripling your traffic.

Chapter 7 - *Creating Forms Fast*: Creating one-off forms—staff surveys, information forms for field trips, informal quizzes—doesn't have to be the webmaster's job. In this chapter, deputize your power users with PloneFormGen, a flexible form-building tool. Make self-validating forms without any coding. Configure them to email their submissions or store them in access-controlled areas of the site for easy group access.

Chapter 8 - *Styling Your Site*: For a fast site launch, nothing beats pulling a ready-made look off the shelf and slapping your logo on it. However, if time permits, a custom look greatly increases your site's cachet. This chapter is a crash course in Plone 3 theme creation. After untangling Plone's confusing theming situation, we walk you through the development of a skeletal theme, giving you everything you need to customize any of Plone's default CSS or images. For more advanced theming, we point you to the best online and print resources.

Chapter 9 - *Going Live*: The quality of your deployment configuration can be the difference between unusably slow and refreshingly brisk. In this chapter, set up a Plone installation that can serve hundreds of anonymous requests per second using one-size-fits-almost-all sample configurations. Configure ZEO clustering to make use of multiple processors. Turn the knobs in CacheFu to achieve the ideal balance between speed and freshness. Use the included Squid configuration to set up the industry-leading caching proxy in minutes. End with a sample Apache virtual host configuration that ties it all together.

Chapter 10 - *Maintenance, Backups, and Upgrades*: Keep Plone running smoothly by automating database maintenance and backups. Ensure pain-free upgrades by learning how much to trust Plone's releases, and test third-party products to avoid unpleasant surprises.

What you need for this book

You should already have Plone installed on your personal machine and become comfortable with its basic facilities: pages, folders, collections, the **Sharing** tab, workflow, and installing add-on products. The majority of this book takes place at this authoring level: no coding required. After all, that's the point of using an off-the-shelf content management system.

> Haven't installed Plone yet? Download it from `http://plone.org/products/plone`. An excellent guide to the basics is the free book, *A User's Guide to Plone*, available at `http://www.plonebook.info/books`.

The chapters *Extending Faculty/Staff Directory* and *Styling Your Site*, whose goals are to build custom add-on products, assume some knowledge of Python. A sprinkling of experience with the Zope framework will also help but is not required; there are plenty of sidebars to bring you up to speed on basic concepts.

> Don't know Python? Don't panic! If you know a few other imperative, block-structured languages, it's a breeze to pick up. The tutorial at `http://docs.python.org/tutorial` will show you the basics without wasting your time, and we promise to comment our code snippets liberally.

The last two chapters, *Going Live* and *Maintenance, Backups, and Upgrades* assume command-line proficiency on the operating system of your choice.

Who this book is for

This book is for webmasters at small schools, web teams at universities looking for a starting point, and enterprising faculties looking to bring their courses to the web. Rather than an in-depth book on coding for Plone, it is designed to help those familiar with Plone at a user or an administrator level in building a useful education-domain site without spending months shopping for add-on products or determining best practices through trial and error.

A word about Information Architecture

This book doesn't presume to dictate one Information Architecture to rule them all; the right IA for your school or department can really only be designed with its particular audience and mission in mind. (For a great primer on IA, see Peter Morville and Louis Rosenfeld's *Information Architecture for the World Wide Web*.) However, most chapters are peppered with observations of what has and has not worked, gleaned from experience with dozens of educational Plone sites.

Conventions

In this book, we use a number of text styles to denote different kinds of information. Here are the styles and their meanings:

Bits of code within larger blocks of text are styled like this: "`repozo`, a tool included in the `bin` directory, makes incremental backups easy."

A block of code is set as follows:

```
[buildout]
eggs =
    ...(other eggs)...
    Products.FacultyStaffDirectory
```

When we wish to draw your attention to a particular part of a code block, the relevant lines or items are set in bold:

```
[buildout]
eggs =
    ...(other eggs)...
    Products.FacultyStaffDirectory
```

Any command-line input or output is written as follows:

```
paster create -t plone3_buildout my_plone_3_buildout
```

New terms and **important words** are shown in bold. Words that you see on the screen, in menus or dialog boxes for example, appear in the text like this: "When in quick-edit mode, you'll see a **Form Actions** table below the list of fields."

[Warnings or important notes appear in a box like this.]

[Tips and tricks appear like this.]

Reader feedback

Feedback from our readers is always welcome. Let us know what you think about this book—what you liked or disliked. Reader feedback is important for us to develop titles that help you the most.

To send us general feedback, email us at `feedback@packtpub.com`, and mention the book title in the subject of your message.

If there is a book that you need and would like to see us publish, please send us a note using the **SUGGEST A TITLE** form on `www.packtpub.com`, or email `suggest@packtpub.com`.

If there is a topic that you have expertise in and you are interested in either writing or contributing to a book on, see our author guide on `www.packtpub.com/authors`.

Customer support

Now that you are the proud owner of a Packt book, we have a number of things to help you to get the most from your purchase.

[Downloading the example code for the book

Visit `http://www.packtpub.com/files/code/8129_Code.zip` to directly download the example code.

The downloadable files contain instructions on how to use them.]

Errata

Although we have taken every care to ensure the accuracy of our content, mistakes do happen. If you find a mistake in this book—in the text or the code—we would be grateful if you would report it to us. By doing so, you can save other readers frustration and help us to improve subsequent versions of this book. If you find any errors, please report them by visiting `http://www.packtpub.com/support`, selecting this book, clicking on the **let us know** link, and entering the details of the error. Once verified, your submission will be accepted, and the correction added to any list of existing errata. Existing errata can be viewed by selecting your title at `http://www.packtpub.com/support`.

Piracy

Piracy of copyright material on the Internet is an ongoing problem across all media. At Packt, we take the protection of our copyright and licenses very seriously. If you come across any illegal copies of our works, in any form, on the Internet, please send the location, address, or web site name to `copyright@packtpub.com` so we can pursue a remedy.

We appreciate your help in protecting our authors and our ability to bring you valuable content.

Questions

You can contact us at `questions@packtpub.com` if you have a problem with any aspect of the book, and we will do our best to address it.

1
Creating Courses

If you use Plone for your school's public web presence or intranet, it might also make sense to use it for your courses:

- Courses can interact naturally with other Plone content. For example, an event listing can combine exams and athletics.
- Plone is more customizable than commercial offerings like WebCT or Blackboard, and there's no worry about another company swallowing it.
- Plone can save hundreds of thousands of dollars per year over a commercial course management system.
- Consistent navigation and one-stop search come for free, avoiding the need to cobble together disparate systems with arcane web server rewrite rules.
- Plone brings flexible access control and workflow, freedom from the webmaster bottleneck, and the other general advantages listed in the Preface.

There isn't a lot of support specifically for doing course management in Plone. However, there is plenty of overlap between course management and the more general content management at which Plone excels. With creative application of content types, Plone can make a respectable showing against some of the most popular course management packages: you get events, discussion forums, custom forms for online testing, assignment submission, and a flexible permission system for enabling collaboration, along with the integration and consistency advantages of a single system.

This chapter suggests a flexible strategy for representing courses using Plone's built-in content types—news items, collections, and events—all without a single line of code. We'll put course materials online, publish assignments and announcements, and lay the groundwork for add-ons like blogs, forums, and other third-party products covered in later chapters. Following the iterative philosophy of beginning with the simplest approach that adds value, we'll keep away from markup and stylesheet tweaks for now; what we build will be functional and reasonably attractive, so you can put the basics into production fast, returning later to sand off the rough edges with a third-party theme or a bit of custom coding.

Finally, while the following strategies are one set of working practices, don't be afraid to mold them to your school's needs. Customization is Plone's strong suit!

Prepare a place for courses

Our first order of business is deciding where to store courses. Instructors using Plone on their own sometimes create an entire Plone site for each course. While this lets them choose add-on products on a per-course basis and offers some isolation should a catastrophe occur, it carries two important disadvantages:

- *A maintenance burden.* Unless you are adept at writing scripts to automate it, upgrading and editing redundant settings on several Plone sites takes time and invites error.
- *An integration challenge.* Sharing information among Plone sites is tricky. By using a single site, you get integrated navigation and search without having to cobble together bridging solutions using XML-RPC or RSS.

Thus, we recommend keeping all your courses (and whatever else you can get away with politically) in a single Plone site. We will keep the courses in a special kind of folder called a **large folder**.

Folders versus Large Folders

In Plone 3, there are two main types of folders—**folders** and **large folders**—each with its own advantages.

Folders are best for holding less than about fifty items. Their contents can be manually ordered through drag-and-drop and appear beneath their enclosing folder in Navigation portlets. However, whenever a folder is loaded into memory (**unpickled**, in Python parlance), all its contents are loaded as well. This takes up a lot of RAM and causes slowdowns if folders are overpopulated. In addition, since folders store all their contents in a single Python "tuple", they are a prime source of **conflict errors** in Zope's database: temporary errors which happen whenever two transactions try to write to the same object at once. In addition to adding noise to your error logs, these hurt performance, since they require the entire transaction—everything done in response to the HTTP request—to be redone.

Large folders, on the other hand, are optimized to hold thousands of items, storing their contents in a B-tree, a data structure that supports incremental loading and therefore needs less RAM and disk access. B-trees also provide finer-grained locking, making for fewer conflict errors. The downside is that their contents cannot be manually ordered. Also, for cosmetic reasons, their contents aren't listed in Navigation portlets (though this can be changed in the `portal_types` tool in the ZMI).

A note about the future

In Plone 4, both folder types will be subsumed by a hybrid that combines the best attributes of each. Called `plone.folder`, this package is, as of October 2009, available separately for Plone 3 at beta quality. If you choose to use it now, migration to the Plone 4 version will likely be smooth.

Enable large folders

Large folders are not available from the **Add new** menu (**addable**) out of the box. To enable them…

1. Go to **Site Setup** → **Zope Management Interface**, colloquially known as "the **ZMI**." This is an under-the-hood view for tweaking infrequently used settings and performing advanced tasks.
2. Go to **portal_types** → **Large Plone Folder**, where you can control the behavior of the Large Folder type within the Plone site.
3. Turn on **Implicitly addable**, and save. Large folders are can now be added throughout the site.

Once you are finished adding large folders, it's a good idea to revoke their addability to prevent user confusion. Otherwise, users will see them in their **Add** menus.

Create the "Courses" folder

Next, create a top-level large folder for holding courses:

1. Navigate back to the top level of your Plone site (no longer in the ZMI), and choose **Add new → Large Folder**. Title it "Courses," and save. (Now is a great time to return to `portal_types` and turn off large folder addability.)

   Although large folders are supposedly designed to hold thousands of items, their views are unpaginated: they are happy to display all those thousands of items on one gigantic page. Improving this behavior is on the docket for a future version of Plone: `http://dev.plone.org/plone/ticket/9544`. In the meantime, we can take advantage of a little trick using collections to add pagination to the folder:

2. Inside the **Courses** folder, choose **Add new → Collection**. Title it "Courses" like its surrounding folder, so the name of the folder and the title on its default page are consistent. Save it.

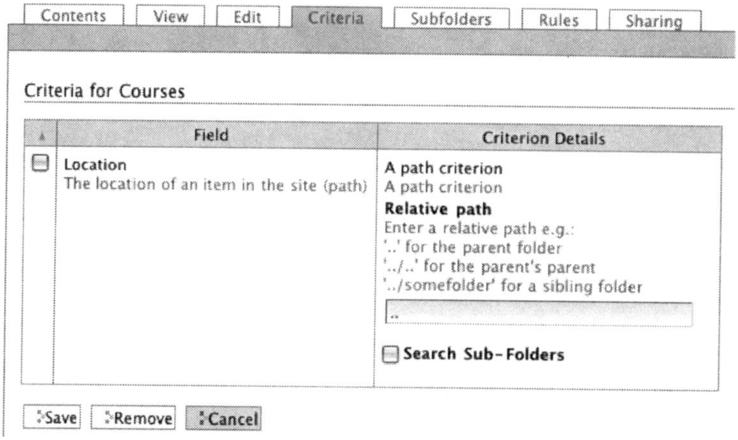

3. On the collection's **Criteria** tab, add a relative **Location** criterion, and leave.. (the default) as its **Relative path**. **Search Sub-Folders** should remain unchecked; we want to pull in only the direct contents of the Courses folder.

4. Under **Set Sort Order**, select **Title** to make courses appear in alphabetical order.

5. Go back to the collection's **View** tab, and choose **Display → Summary view**. This keeps users from seeing distracting author information and modification dates.
6. On the collection's **Edit → Dates** tab, set the **Publishing Date** far in the future. This ugly but effective trick keeps the collection from showing up in the folder listing for students. You will still see it, however, since you created it.
7. Finally, navigate back to the **Courses** folder, and set the collection as its default view: choose **Display → Select a content item as default view**, and choose the **Courses** collection.

Congratulations! Perhaps that seemed a lot of work for an empty folder, but pagination and efficient storage are insurance against being woken in the middle of the night when your server chokes trying to render too many 1,000-course pages. (It also means fewer servers to buy, a significant monetary saving for your institution.)

Incidentally, you can feel free to add additional levels of organization within your Courses folder at this point: for example, grouping courses by subject or level. Just remember to revoke large folder addability when you're done.

Create the course skeleton

Now that we have a full-featured container, let's add an example course.

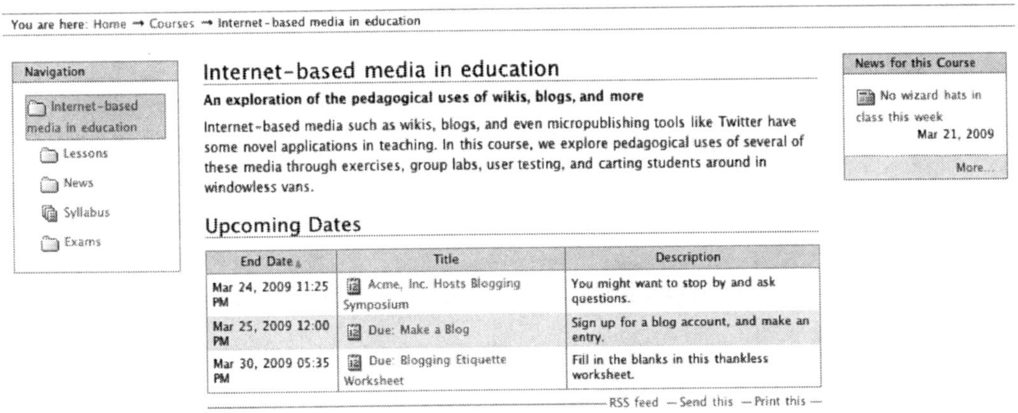

A simple folder is the root of our course:

1. Add a folder within the Courses folder. Set its title to the name of our example course, "Internet-based media in education."

Several folders within provide spots for other content:

2. Create a Lessons folder within your course. Set its **Display** to **Summary view** to hide distracting authorship information and modification dates.
3. Head back to the "Internet-based media in education" folder that represents your course, and make an Exams folder. The "Exams" categorization won't necessarily make sense for every course, but it is an example of where to put calendar events unassociated with any specific lesson.
4. Ascend back to the "Internet-based media in education" folder, and make a News folder, a home for announcements that should not appear on the site's calendars and other by-date listings.

Now that we have a skeleton of a course, we can flesh out the component folders with example content.

Add a lesson

The Lessons folder we created above holds lectures, chapters, units—any divisions of course material that have associated assignments. Here we'll create a sample lesson about blogs in the "Internet-based media in education" course:

1. Create a folder inside the Lessons folder to represent the lesson. Title it "Blogs".
2. Create a Page called "Blogs" inside the Blogs folder. It will act as the front page of the lesson and hold most of the instructional content.
3. On that Page's **Edit** → **Settings** tab, turn on **Table of contents** and **Allow comments**.
4. Returning to the Blogs folder, use the **Display** menu to make the Blogs page its default view.

The value of comments

It's just one checkbox, but allowing comments on a lesson can be a great help to students and teachers alike.

- Comments invite feedback from students while they are using the material, capturing reactions that might be lost if left until the next class meeting. Instructors can use this information to better adjust the pace and content of courses.
- Comments provide a more permanent record of trends than fleeting verbal inquiries, which is helpful when revising a course between semesters.
- Written comments are more accessible to students who are uncomfortable asking questions aloud, such as non-native English speakers.
- Comments increase student-to-student interaction. Some classes even become self-supporting, with students answering each other's questions. If this becomes popular in your classes, you may want to explore a more full-featured solution; see the discussion of Ploneboard in the *Blogs and Forums* chapter.

Finally, a word about comment abuse: there doesn't tend to be much, at least among college-age students. Since only logged-in users can add comments by default, "social access control" kicks in: students are reticent to dole out abuse when identified by name to their peers and professors.

Lesson materials: one page or many?

In this example lesson, most of the instructional material lives on a single page (set as the lesson folder's default view), with a dynamically generated table of contents supporting in-page navigation. Consider breaking it into multiple pages if…

- …a lesson is so large that navigating within a single page becomes clumsy.
- …there are smaller concepts within the lesson that would be useful for other pages to link to.

- ...you anticipate a clean division of comment topics. For example, if your lesson is about matrix mathematics and covers both Eigenvalues and the use of MATLAB to compute them, you might expect comments to divide into questions about the math and questions about MATLAB. Splitting the lesson into separate pages along those lines will help keep comments naturally divided as well, improving organization and navigation.

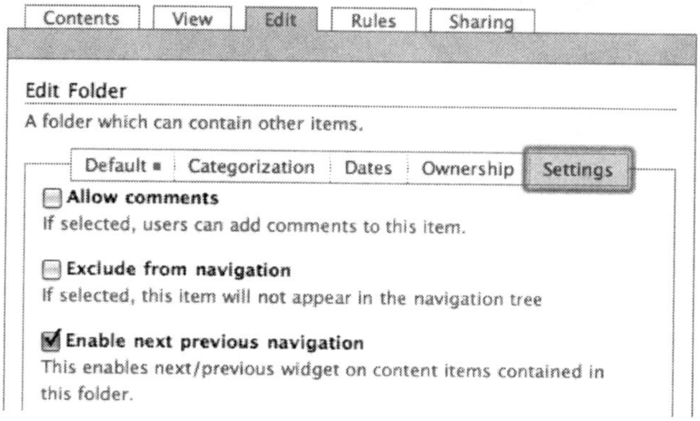

Remember that Plone can generate next/previous links automatically: just find the folder representing the lesson, and check the **Enable next previous navigation** box on its **Edit** → **Settings** tab.

Add an assignment to the lesson

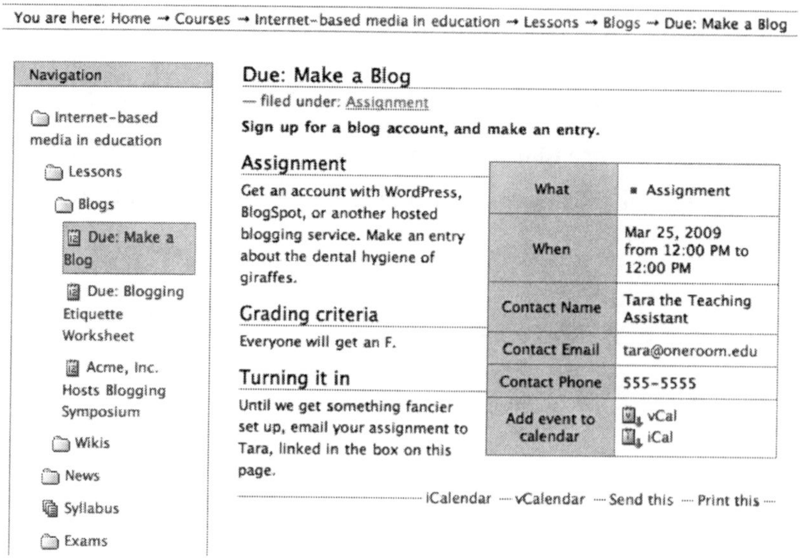

Plone's Event type is a good choice for almost anything associated with a date and time. With a little ingenuity, we can repurpose it to represent assignments with due dates. Here's how to add an assignment represented by an event:

1. Add an event inside the Blogs folder.
2. Title it something like "Due: Make a Blog". Beginning assignment events with "Due: " lets them coexist in listings with other types of events without being confused with non-assignments, like group work sessions on similar topics. "Due" is also easy to visually scan for, since it is always in the same place in an assignment's title; while "Blogging Assignment Due" would also be semantically correct, it would be trickier to pick out of a list.
3. Set both **Event Starts** and **Event Ends** to the time and date the assignment is due. This will position it properly on calendars and lists without any question of which end of the span represents the due time.
4. Set the **Event Type(s)** to "Assignment" so something other than a blank table cell shows up opposite the "What" label on the assignment's page. This also gives us a handy keyword to search against later. Experience has shown this step is the easiest to forget, so be sure to stress it when training content contributors.
5. The **Event body text** is a perfect place for the assignment details.
6. As with lessons, above, turning on **Settings → Allow comments** is a fantastic way to encourage student interaction with instructors and each other. Instructors will appreciate the emergence of student-to-student support here, as it lets them concentrate more time on the difficult questions.

   In the *Blogs and Forums* chapter, we'll take commenting to the next level by adding a full-fledged discussion forum to each assignment.
7. The **Contact Name** and **Contact Phone** fields are convenient places to delegate support duties to a teaching assistant, if needed.
8. As a simple hand-in mechanism, specify a **Contact E-mail**, and direct assignment submissions there. This field provides spam armoring that is quite effective in practice: `mailto:tara@oneroom.edu` becomes `mail to:tara@oneroom.edu`, which has so far been enough to make the spam spiders move along to easier targets. Note that simply embedding a `mailto` link in the event's body text doesn't take advantage of the armoring.

   For a more sophisticated turn-in form, see the *Creating Forms Fast* chapter, where you'll find everything you need to construct a full-fledged submission form.

Add course-wide events

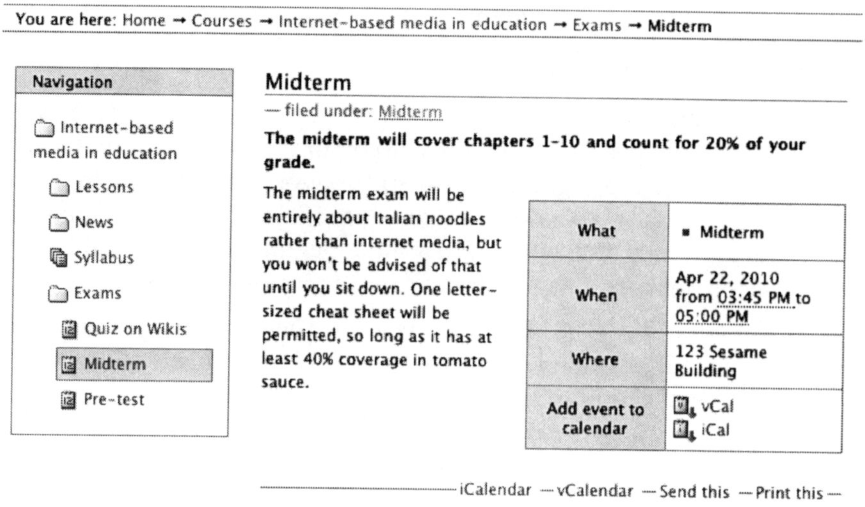

Most courses include some events that aren't associated with any specific lesson: for example, exams. We created an Exams folder earlier, and we'll now flesh it out with a collection that orders and displays its contents:

1. Add a collection to the Exams folder. Title it "Exams" so it appears consistent when used as the folder's default view.
2. On the **Criteria** tab, add a **Location** criterion, and choose **Criteria type** → **Location in site relative to the current location**.
3. Leave **Relative path** as its default two dots. This makes the collection return everything in the Exams folder.
4. Turn **Search Sub-Folders** on so that, if an instructor accumulates enough exams to warrant the use of subfolders, the main Exams folder will still act as a flattened chronological listing. This saves students from having to dig through the folder hierarchy.
5. Click the first **Save** button on the page (not the second).
6. On the collection's **View** tab, choose **Display** → **Summary view** to hide the unnecessary authorship information.
7. Return to the Exams folder, and use the **Display** menu to make your new collection the default view.

Feel free to make additional folders that hold non-lesson-specific events. In our example, you might have a folder listing local speaking engagements by prominent bloggers.

> **Creating collections can be confusing**
>
> As you may now appreciate, the user interface for editing collections is a bit hard to follow. When delegating privileges to content contributors, you may wish to withhold the ability to create collections from all but the most proficient users. This can cut down on visitors being frustrated by collections that don't do quite what they expect.

Use news items for course-specific announcements

The course-wide News folder behaves similarly to the Exams folder, the main difference being that its contents should not appear on calendars. This folder is a fine place for non-date-sensitive announcements such as "The grading curve has been adjusted" or "Found: one blue vinyl purse".

To set up the News folder, follow a similar recipe as for the Exams folder:

1. Add a collection to the **News** folder. Call it "News."
2. On the **Criteria** tab, add a **Location** criterion, and choose **Criteria type → Location in site relative to the current location**.
3. Set **Relative path** to "**../..**" (without the quotation marks). This makes the collection start its search at the root of the course.
4. Turn **Search Sub-Folders** on so the collection will return all the news items in the entire course, not just at its top level.
5. Click the first **Save** button on the page (not the second).
6. On the collection's **View** tab, choose **Display → Summary view** to hide the authorship information.
7. Return to the News folder, and use the **Display** menu to set your new collection as the default view.

Add a course news portlet

The main attraction on the front page will be a list of assignment due dates, but announcements are in second place. Since Plone cannot include two collections in the main content area without custom templating and our goal is to perform this task entirely code-free, we list the news in a portlet.

The News portlet that ships with Plone searches the entire site, which makes it not ideal when storing multiple courses per site. Fortunately, it's straightforward to make a Collection portlet do the same job with a tighter scope. In fact, we can re-use the collection we defined above:

1. Navigate to the folder that represents your course, and click **Manage portlets**.
2. Choose **Add portlet...** → **Collection portlet**.
3. Set the **Portlet header** to "News for this Course," which makes its scope clear.
4. Set the **Target collection** to the **News** collection within the course's **News** folder.
5. Set **Limit** to about 5, depending on the course's expected rate of news flow.
6. Turn on **Show dates** to add a little context to each item.

Collect due dates on the course's front page

Most visitors to a course come looking for homework assignments, so we place them front and center. We can display them on the front page by the now-familiar trick of using a collection as a folder's default view:

1. Add a collection to the folder that represents your course. Give it the same title as the course itself.
2. Enter a short description of the course under **Description**.
3. If you like, put a slightly more lengthy summary of the course under **Body Text**. Experience indicates that the summary is often ignored, so make it expendable. Also, keep the summary short so the due dates aren't hidden at the bottom of the page, which could be scrolled out of view.
4. End the **Body Text** field with an "Upcoming Dates" heading, which will function as a heading for the collection results below.
5. Check **Display as Table**. Choose the table columns **End Date**, **Description**, and **Title**, and save.
6. Head over to the collection's **Criteria** tab. Add an **End Date** criterion that lists **Which day** as **2 weeks**, **In the past or future** as **in the future**, and **More or less** as **Less than**. This cryptic piece of configuration should show events with end dates two or fewer weeks in the future.
7. Add an **Item Type** criterion set to **Event**.

8. Add a relative **Location** criterion with a **Relative path** of .. and **Search Sub-Folders** on.

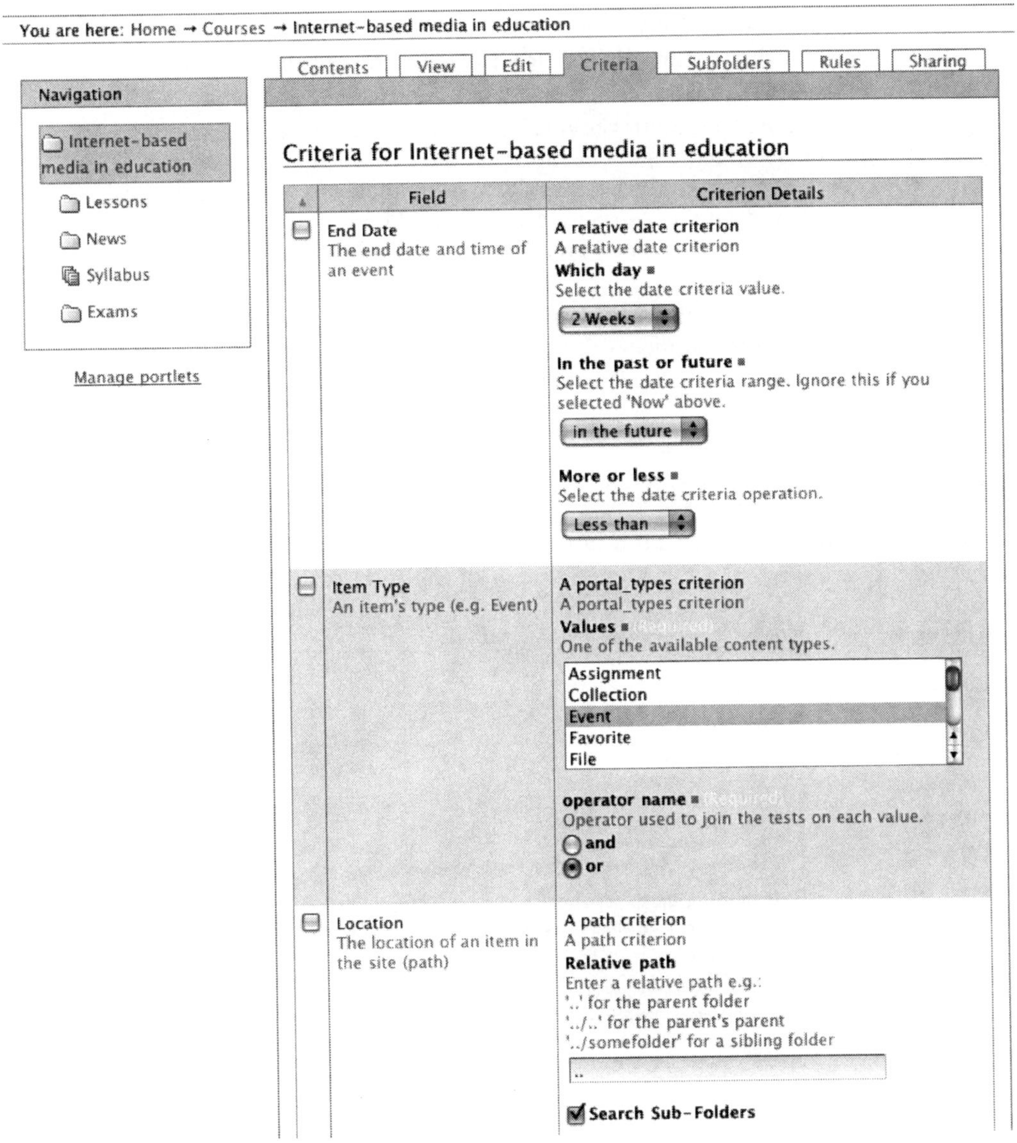

9. Set the collection as the default view of the course.

> **Keep students up to date with RSS**
>
> Students are not in the habit of visiting course web pages to check for updates. But, with a bit of prompting, they can be convinced to subscribe to their courses using **RSS**, a protocol for automatically retrieving site updates.
>
> In Plone, all collections provide RSS feeds, and in our course framework, the course's front-page collection provides a particularly useful one. It collects items from the Exams folder, assignments from all lessons, and any other event the instructor sees fit to add within the course. Add to this the **News** collection, and you have a fairly comprehensive source of updates.
>
> However, most students—even technically savvy ones—have no idea what RSS is, so a quick walkthrough of a web-based client like Google Reader can be a handy thing to add to your site and reference from syllabi.

Add a syllabus

A course's syllabus is important but not nearly as popular as the latest homework assignment, so we make it a top-level member of the course, though not its front page.

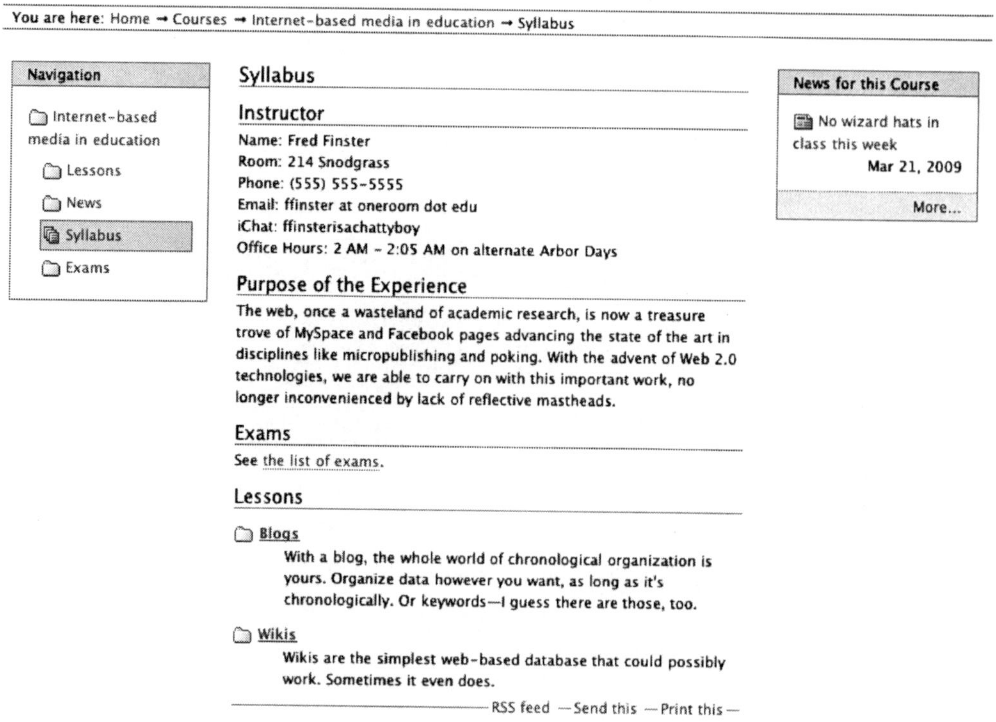

1. At the root of the course, add a collection titled "Syllabus".
2. In the **Body Text** field, enter the bulk of the course's syllabus: instructor contact information, the goals of the course, a link to the Exams folder, and, finally, a hanging "Lessons" heading. Links to the RSS feeds of the front-page collection and the News collection are also good additions. Once you are satisfied with your syllabus text, click **Save**.

   If you set up a personnel directory as in the *Showcasing Personnel with Faculty/Staff Directory* chapter, replace the instructor contact info with a link to his or her directory entry so there is a single place to update it.
3. Head to the **Criteria** tab, and add a relative **Location** criterion with a **Relative path** of **../lessons**. This will pull in all the top-level contents of the Lessons folder. Presto! Assuming you wrote good descriptions for your lessons, you have an instant course summary.

Reusing the course framework

Now that you have one functioning course, you can create more just by copying and pasting it. Make a spare course, fill it with just enough example material to inspire instructors, set it to the Private workflow state so no one sees it, and you're all ready to populate your entire course catalog.

Summary

In this chapter, we have created a miniature course management framework scalable to thousands of courses. We have...

- Places for lesson materials, assignments, and calendar events
- A course front page that automatically displays the latest homework assignments and announcements
- A syllabus that gathers a course summary from individual lesson descriptions
- An easy way to keep students up to date with RSS

We've also touched on a few points of pedagogy and information architecture, like the impact of online comments on a class.

Where to go from here

If you are in a hurry to get a course management solution up and running, you might want to skip ahead to...

- The *Styling Your Site* chapter if you are satisfied with this functionality but want to improve the markup or CSS a bit
- The *Creating Forms Fast* chapter if you would like to add more sophisticated turn-in capabilities
- The *Blogs and Forums* chapter if you need those content types
- The *Calendaring* chapter to explore more ways of displaying and filtering events

2
Calendaring

In Chapter 1, *Creating Courses*, we used events to represent due dates and exams and reorganized them dynamically using collections. But your school's use of events will likely span athletics, music performances, conferences, and much more.

In this chapter, we embark on a deeper study of Plone events, seeing how to...

- Harness the best-of-breed Plone4Artists Calendar product to improve the display of event listings
- Gather events from across a site into a central calendar, culling out class-specific due dates and assignments
- Let visitors browse a single hierarchy of events arranged by subject while still allowing edit permissions to be delegated along organization boundaries
- Represent recurring events

The techniques in this chapter are applicable in many organizational schemes. We present one common arrangement as an example: a top-level folder where visitors can browse the highest-profile events on the site.

Show events on a calendar

Plone's out-of-the-box **Events** folder provides a basic way to find events: it displays them in a chronological list broken into pages of 20 each. While fine for simple cases, this is cumbersome for visitors who want to look at events for a certain future date. Part of our goal is to set up a monthly calendar to make this common case easy:

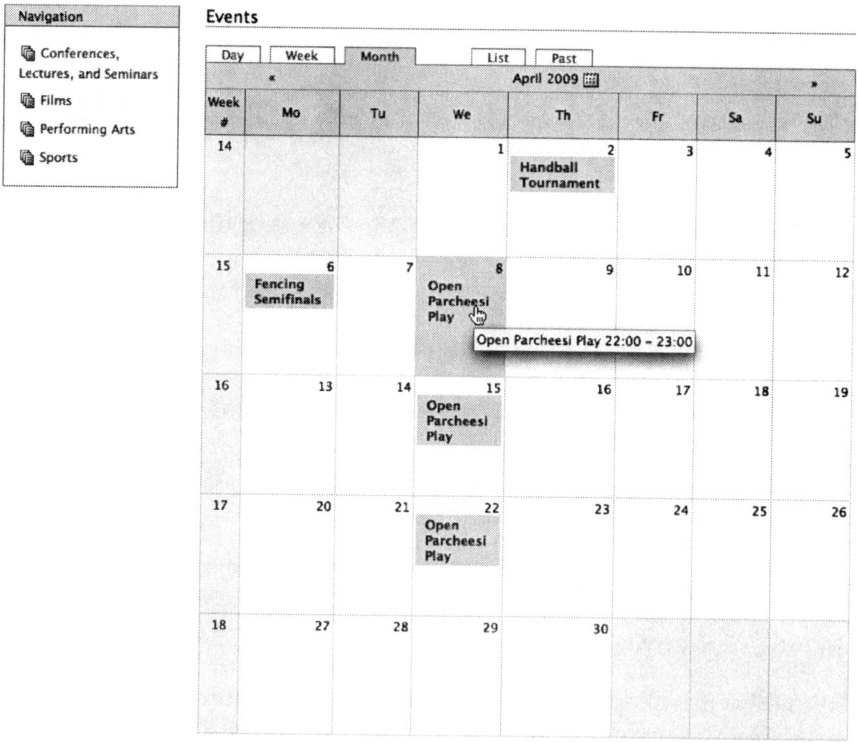

Our first step toward the monthly calendar is to replace Plone's stock **Events** folder. Out of the box, it holds individual events along with a summarizing collection that acts as its front page. If you don't need a drill-down way of browsing your events by subject—for example, if you have so few that they all fit comfortably on a calendar like the above—you can leave the default **Events** folder in place. Otherwise, follow the instructions below to replace it with a standalone collection; this will interact better with Plone's navigation portlet, which we will use to implement the drill-down browsing. If you choose to stick with the stock **Events** folder, you may still wish to adjust the criteria of its inner collection as described in the following:

1. First, delete the **Events** folder.
2. Replace it with a new collection called "Events". Give it an **Item Type** criterion, and tell it to pull in everything of the type **Event**.

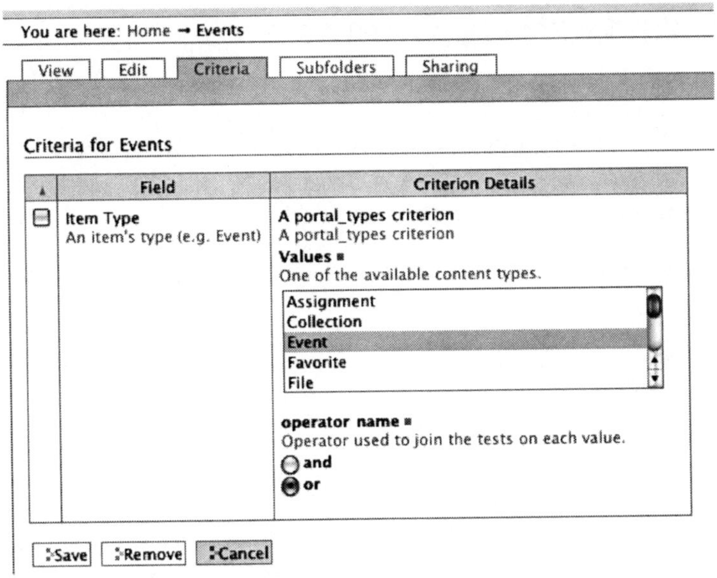

The original **Events** collection had a **Start Date** criterion to keep past events off the page. We won't need that, since the calendar view we are about to apply keeps past events tucked away implicitly—and we do want the ability to see old events when we navigate to previous months.

The original collection also had a **State** criterion that limited it to showing published events. If you need only to hide unpublished events from visitors, then you can dispense with this: the internal search routines used by the collection will naturally show only what the current user has permission to see.

> **Preventing a common contributor error**
>
> Often, a less proficient contributor will add an event, see it on his or her own calendar, and move on, neglecting to publish it. Adding the **State** criterion can serve as a reminder, preventing the event from appearing until properly published. The downside is that it makes the calendar useless for intranets: Events that aren't publicly visible will never show up. But if you have no non-public events to list, consider recreating the **State** criterion.

3. If you never want to show access-controlled events on the main calendar add a **State** criterion limiting the collection to published items.

The **Events** collection is finished. Next, we apply a monthly calendar view to our data.

Meet Plone4Artists Calendar

Plone's built-in event listings are rather basic. As we saw in *Creating Courses*, we need to do special tricks with collections and default views just to sort them in chronological order. At best, this is several extra clicks, and, at worst, it can confuse your less technical content contributors. A third-party product called Plone4Artists Calendar makes this easy and gives us several other capabilities to boot.

Plone4Artists Calendar is the current frontrunner in the Plone calendaring space. It provides…

- Daily, weekly, monthly, and a few other calendar-like views for folders and collections
- Rudimentary recurring event support
- Hooks for pulling events from other systems in realtime, with a bit of coding

Don't let the name "Plone4Artists" put you off if you aren't an artist; though the Plone4Artists suite of products came out of a project to provide artist community web sites, there's nothing particularly artist-centric about them. In fact, there has been discussion about renaming them.

The runner up: CalendarX

The other Plone calendar worth considering is CalendarX, whose most recent release at the time of this writing is 0.9.1. 0.9.0 was the first update to the product since since 2005 and represents a major refit. Its ancient data-modeling internals were replaced with a modern Archetypes implementation, and one no longer needed to venture into the ZMI to do simple configuration. Speaking of configuration, CalendarX exposes a *lot* of it: 6 tabs packed with options for tweaking calendar format, event display, widgets, and more. There are 57 options alone regarding its CSS cosmetics. If you need a specific look and aren't comfortable writing your own CSS or template code, CalendarX may be the ticket.

However, be warned that CalendarX has a history of being sporadically maintained. It lacked Plone 3 compatibility for a long time, and compatibility work began only when a group of stranded Plone 2.5 users at Pennsylvania State University put a week of development work toward it. Its internals still hold a lot of legacy that may prove difficult to maintain as Plone evolves.

Plone4Artists Calendar, on the other hand, is a simpler product—both inside and outside and with all the good and bad that entails—and the winds of further community effort are blowing in its direction. Its maintainable design and the willingness of developers to work on it make it the solution least likely to leave you stranded; this is why it is our recommendation in this chapter.

Install Plone4Artists Calendar

Before we can make use of its views, we need to install the product—actually, two products and several supporting packages. Weave these directives into the proper sections of your `buildout.cfg`...

```
[buildout]
...other directives...
eggs =
    ...other eggs here...
    p4a.plonecalendar
    p4a.ploneevent

[instance]
...other directives...
zcml =
    ...other ZCML listings here...
    # Plone4Artists Calendar doesn't support Plone 3.3's auto-ZCML-
loading as of 2.0a2.
    p4a.plonecalendar-meta
    p4a.plonecalendar
    p4a.ploneevent

[productdistros]
recipe = plone.recipe.distros
urls =
   http://plone.org/products/calendaring/releases/0.4/
calendaring-0-4-0.tgz
```

...run buildout, restart Zope/Plone, and install the **Plone4ArtistsCalendar** (**p4a.plonecalendar**) and **Recurring Events** (**p4a.ploneevent**) products in **Site Setup** → **Add-on Products**.

Now that everything is installed, we apply a monthly calendar view to the **Events** collection:

1. Navigate back to the **Events** collection, and choose **Calendar** from the new **Sub-types** menu.
2. If it isn't already selected, choose **Month** view from the **Display** menu.

Presto—we have a monthly calendar showing every event on our site.

Exclude trivia from the site-wide calendar

Of course, we don't really want every event; for any but the smallest sites, this would quickly crowd the calendar to uselessness. We would like to limit the site-wide calendar to the most noteworthy events, omitting specialty items like assignments that apply to only one in a hundred people. (For that matter, typical visitors won't think of assignments as "events" at all and would be surprised to see them on the calendar.) There are several ways to indicate an event's noteworthiness without resorting to much coding:

- Copy the Event type to make a new but identical type called something like "Site-Wide Event", either by writing a product or by simply copying and pasting within the `portal_types` tool, accessed through **Site Setup → Zope Management Interface**. Have the **Events** collection find only instances of the new type. When considering this approach, note that an Events portlet will show only events of the original type. A partial workaround is to use a Collection portlet instead.
- Assign certain folders in the site to hold noteworthy events, then gather them with a collection: a **Location in site** criterion easily brings together the contents of multiple folders.
- Apply a single keyword, such as "Site-Wide Event", to worthy events. Have the **Events** collection pull in only events tagged with that keyword.
- Promote many keywords to the site-wide calendar. Whether you can get away with this depends on your information architecture and the size of your organization. However, if your keywords are used for anything other than contrived purposes like this, your content contributors will likely run into places where one of the promoted keywords is semantically appropriate while showing the event on the site-wide calendar isn't.

Choose one of the above filtering approaches based on the needs of your site, and add a criterion to your **Events** collection to match. If in doubt, use the "Site-Wide Event"-keyword approach.

Build a browsable hierarchy with collections

Even with the earlier pruning, a large school may still have too many events to comfortably view. For example, finding the next few months' varsity football games could be tricky when they're mixed in with all the other sporting events. To make this easier, we build a tree of collections so visitors can drill level-by-level into your taxonomy, homing in on their goal. As they descend, the monthly calendar view continually pares itself down until they reach a number of events they can comfortably comb through:

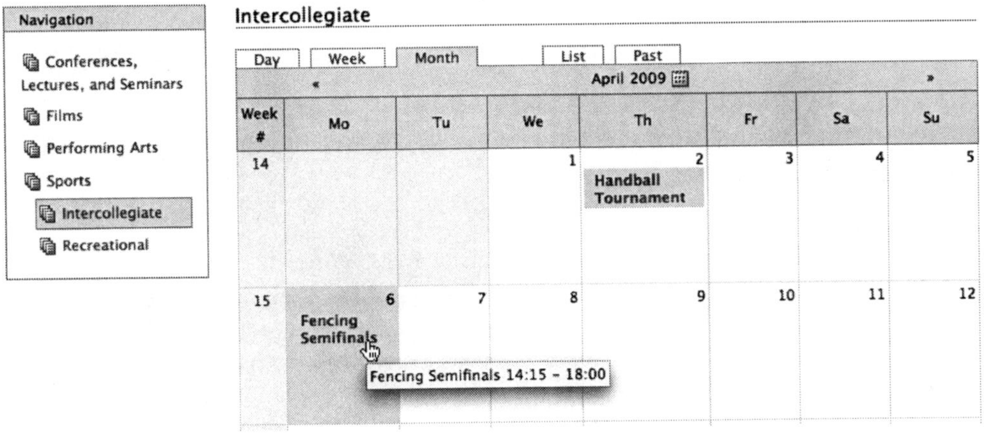

To add one of these drill-down categories, follow these steps:

1. Add a collection inside the Events collection, called, for example, "Sports". Turn on **Inherit Criteria** so this collection becomes a paring down of the one containing it. Save.
2. To make the monthly calendar view persist while visitors drill, choose **Calendar** from the new collection's **Sub-types** menu.

3. Add a **Categories** criterion to the collection to narrow the selection of events. The figure below shows one way to fake a hierarchy of keywords: the **Sports** collection displays events tagged with any of the two sports-related keywords.

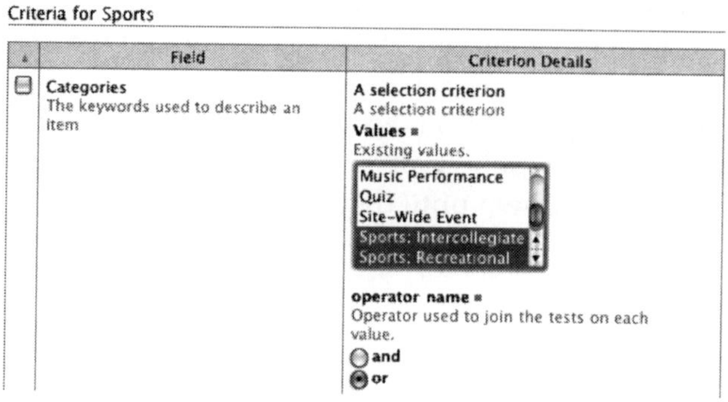

Continue adding second-level and lower sub-collections until the lowest ones all show a manageable number of events.

> **Separating security from information architecture**
>
> Note that the actual location of events in the site is independent of where they are presented to the user. This has important security implications: you can use Plone's location-based access control—setting per-folder roles using the **Sharing** tab—without having to give anyone total write access to an all-encompassing Sports folder. This lets you treat security according to your organization's administrative structure while insulating site visitors from it.

> **Embracing local security**
>
> A common error made by new Plone administrators is to assign a lot of privileges through the checkboxes in the **Users and Groups Administration** control panel. In practice, these should hardly be used at all. Though prominently placed, they grant privileges across the entire site, and not many people need such power. We recommend using them only to give Manager rights to the sort of people who have root access to the web server: a small cadre of trusted webmasters and sysadmins.
>
> Instead, assign most permissions through the **Sharing** tabs on individual folders. And, when information architecture doesn't specify otherwise, structure your folder hierarchy to take advantage of the fact that items inherit the permissions settings of their containers. Where information architecture does conflict with this, there is an easy solution: just turn off the **Sharing** tab's **Inherit Permissions** checkbox and start your role assignments from a blank slate.

Reorder subfolders the hard (but only) way

Controlling the order in which a collection's subfolders appear is often desirable—for example, to maintain alphabetization—but there is no obvious way: subfolders always appear in order of their creation, and there are no reordering controls on the **Subfolders** tab. However, changing the order is possible, if somewhat tedious. First, visit the Zope Management Interface at the level of the outer collection; for example, visit `http://127.0.0.1:8080/your-plone-site/events/manage` to reorder the subfolders of the top-level **Events** collection. Next, select an item or items you would like to move lower in the ordering, cut them, and paste them. Return to a Plone view of the collection, and notice that they have in fact moved. Continue this manual sorting until everything is properly ordered. It's painstaking, but it works.

Incidentally, we have filed an enhancement request at `http://dev.plone.org/plone/ticket/9109`. Check that ticket to see whether the situation has been improved by the time you read this.

Keep keywords clean with Plone Keyword Manager

As the number of keywords in your site increases, keep the third-party Plone Keyword Manager (`http://plone.org/products/plonekeywordmanager`) in mind. Keywords in Plone are site-wide and, like all uncontrolled vocabularies, need a bit of gardening to remain consistent. Keyword Manager lets you merge synonymous keywords without having to manually troll through the whole site. It is a well-maintained product in wide use, so the risk of it breaking your site is slim.

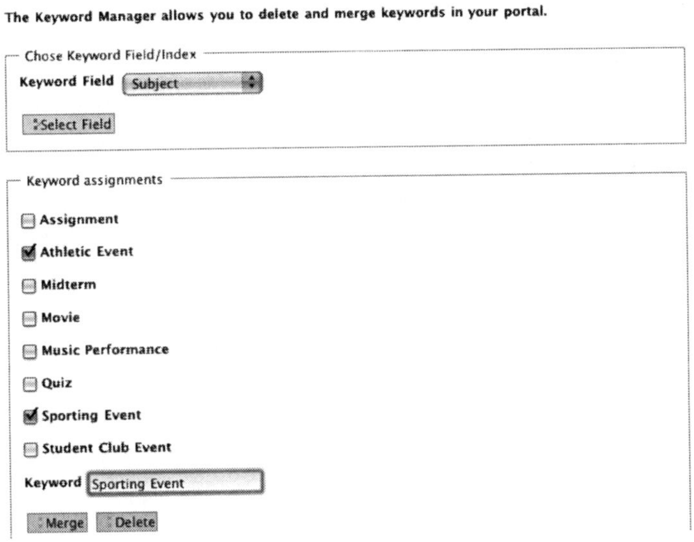

Tips for event contributors

Of course, a calendaring system is no good without a good supply of events. Spare yourself the webmaster bottleneck by farming out event creation to other contributors. Just remember to give them these three tips so your site-wide calendar (and any others you make) are consistent and easy to understand:

- *Name events globally.* It makes sense for the president of the Parcheesi club, adding a night of Parcheesi-filled fun within his own club folder, to name it "Open Play". However, that title doesn't work so well on the site-wide calendar: play of what? Make sure your event contributors understand that "Open Parcheesi Play" is a better title. In addition to making the calendar clear, it will also net visitors more hits when they search for "Parcheesi".
- *Keep dates out of titles.* Because no one can ever get enough Parcheesi, the club offers weekly sessions. It can be tempting, while working in the club's own folder, to differentiate the sessions by adding dates to their titles: "April 15 Open Parcheesi Play". This, of course, is redundant when displayed on a calendar. Steer your contributors away from this practice by showing them how to apply a monthly calendar view even to event folders within clubs.
- *Remember to apply keywords.* Of course, none of this site-wide event aggregation will work unless contributors add keywords to their events. Fortunately, the default event-editing template helps us by prompting for keywords on its main tab, but a little personal encouragement can't hurt either. Also, remember to teach contributors about the "Site-Wide Event" keyword if you decided to use that filtering method.

Represent recurring events

The Recurring Events product, which comes in the `p4a.ploneevent` package, adds the beginnings of repeating event support to Plone, and though it's a bit buggy and in need of user interface work at the moment (such that I wouldn't recommend it for a production site), its underpinnings are well designed. An event can repeat every so many days, weeks, months, or years, and it can stop repeating on a certain date or after some set number of occurrences. Repetition is controlled through a new **Recurrence** tab in the event editor:

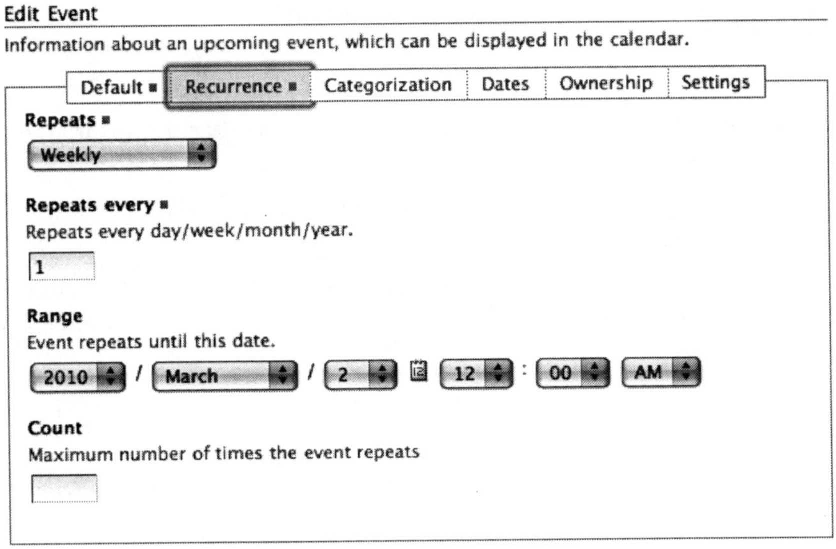

In the above, setting **Repeats every** to 2 would mean "repeat every 2 weeks," with 1 meaning "repeat every week". **Count** means "stop repeating after this many occurrences". If you provide both a **Range** and a **Count**, the most limiting one wins. And although the present interface doesn't support more complex patterns like repeating every Tuesday and Thursday, the underlying `dateutil` library does—so there's plenty of room for future improvement.

Spotty support for showing recurrences

As of `p4a.ploneevent` 0.7.2, event recurrences appear on Plone4Artists Calendar views but not in standard event folder listings. Uninstalling and reinstalling Calendar quietly breaks even the former, so, if you do attempt to use event recurrence, don't plan on reinstalling.

When viewing a single event, the recurrence is rendered in plain English: "**Apr 01, 2009 from 10:55 PM to 11:55 PM Every 2 weeks for 5 times until Mar 02, 2010.**" Unfortunately, the first-ever date of the event always appears instead of the date of its nearest future occurrence. Also, the iCal and vCal downloads are not yet aware of recurrences.

For these and various other reasons, it's probably best to wait until recurring event support is more complete before using it in production sites.

Summary

In this chapter, we have...

- Used Plone4Artists Calendar and collections to gather important events onto a central calendar
- Built a keyword-driven, drill-down navigation scheme for homing in on events by topic
- Made the presentation of events independent of their actual location in the site, letting you take advantage of security inheritance parallel to your organizational structure
- Learned the three things to teach event contributors that will keep your calendar users happy
- Explored the state of Plone4Artists Calendar's recurring event support

3

Showcasing Personnel with Faculty/Staff Directory

It is a rare school that lacks some sort of online personnel directory, whether a public-facing showcase or a private office phone list. The Faculty/Staff Directory product fills both these niches and goes far beyond, letting you...

- Build department- or school-wide directories, collecting contact info, biographies, and more
- Divide people into groups according to their areas of expertise, committee or departmental affiliations, or other organization-specific criteria
- Use those divisions as access-control groups: for example, to grant all the members of a committee access to a private collaboration space
- Write plug-in extenders to track institution-specific pieces of information or hide pieces that don't apply in your organization

Faculty/Staff Directory is practically a departmental web site in a box, but it doesn't stop there. The product is general enough to serve in non-academic settings as well. It is also not limited to people; it has been repurposed to such diverse applications as cataloguing tea leaves. It really is a general-purpose taxonomy engine—albeit with an academic bent in many of its naming choices.

This chapter is an exploration of a product that will likely provide the framework for much of your site. We'll tour its features, get ideas on how they're commonly used in a school setting, and, finally, get a sneak peek into the future of the product.

Install the product

Faculty/Staff Directory depends on several other products: membrane, Relations, and archetypes.schemaextender. Thus, the easiest way to get it, as documented in its readme, is by adding `Products.FacultyStaffDirectory` to your `buildout.cfg`, like so:

```
[buildout]
eggs =
    ...(other eggs)...
    Products.FacultyStaffDirectory
```

Then, shut down Zope, and run buildout.

After starting up Zope again, install `FacultyStaffDirectory` in the **Add-on Products** control panel, and you're ready to go.

Test drive Faculty/Staff Directory

Faculty/Staff Directory (FSD) is tremendously flexible; you can use it as a simple list of phone numbers or as the foundation supporting the rest of your site. In this section, we take FSD for a spin, with ample pit stops along the way to discuss alternative design possibilities. Keep in mind that FSD's features are given to creative repurposing. We'll see not only see their typical uses but some more inventive ones as well.

Create a directory and choose global roles

Faculty/Staff Directory centers around the idea of collecting people in a central folder called, fittingly, a faculty/staff directory. Our first step is to create that folder. Once you've installed FSD in the **Add-on Products** control panel, choose a place in your site where you would like to place a personnel directory, and add a faculty/staff directory there.

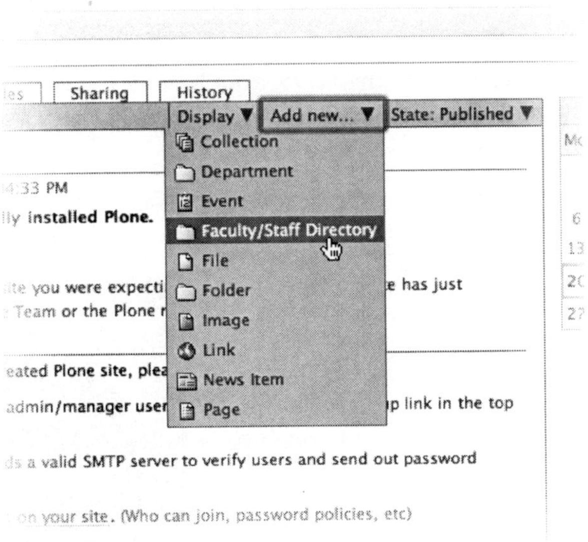

You'll be prompted for two things: **Title** (which is usually something like **People**) and a selection of **Roles**.

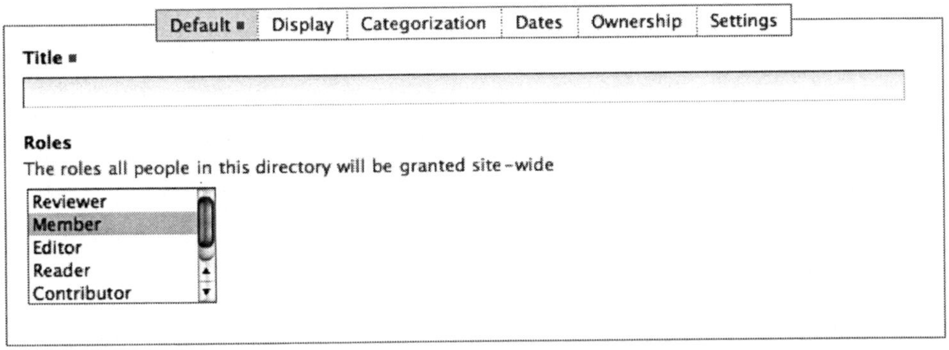

These roles, part of FSD's optional user-and-group integration, are granted site-wide to all people in the directory. Thus, as with the similarly scoped roles in the **Users and Groups** control panel, it's best to use them sparingly: choose only **Member** or, if you don't intend the people represented in your Directory to log in, no roles at all. Most roles should be assigned on a per-folder basis using the **Sharing** tab, and FSD provides facilities for that as well, as we discuss later in the *Integrate users and groups* section.

Add people

Now that you have a place to keep them, it's time to add actual personnel. FSD represents people through the aptly named Person type. A fully tricked-out person might look like this:

Alyssa Trisaha Ph. D

Emil Brahe Professor of Biology

105 Jameson Building
Suite E

College Park , Massachusetts 10049
Email: atrisaha@example.edu
Work: (617) 382-4877

Education:

Ph. D in Hamster Studies from Case Western Reserve

Biography:

Trisaha is the leading researcher in the field of hamster virology today.

Selected Publications:

- Trisaha A, Meane A, Brahms T, Boon R. Four-dimensional Modeling of Hamster Toes with Little Sprinklings of Retrovirus on Top: A Further Abuse of Funding. J Hamst Physio 2001 Nov;51(10):943-54
- Fring QL, Trisaha A, Nishiwaka T, Boon R. Three-dimensional Rendering of Hamster Dance with No Regards for Aesthetics: An Abuse of Funding. J Hamst Physio 2000 Nov;21(12):1379-87

Departments:

Biology Department:
Department Head

Courses:

Endogenous Retroviruses in Hamsters
Origins and research into endogenous retroviruses in modern hamster stock

Prerequisites:

- Guinea Pig Appreciation (GUP 101)
- Mammal-Powered Dynamos (PHY 293)

People, without exception, live directly inside the faculty/staff directory—though they often appear to be elsewhere, as we will soon see. Each person can track the following information:

Basic Information	
Access Account ID	Doubling as the object ID (or "short name") of the person, this field should contain the person's institution-wide login name. If you choose to take advantage of FSD's user-and-group integration, this is how logged-in users are matched with their Person objects. The name of this field and its validation requirements can be changed (and should be, in most deployments) in the **Faculty/Staff Directory** control panel under **Site Setup**.
Name	First, middle, and last names, as well as a suffix such as Ph. D. or Jr.
Image	A picture of the person in GIF, JPEG, or PNG format, for use on their page and in some listings. It will be automatically scaled as necessary.
Classifications	Classifications are FSD's most prominent way to group people. This is a convenient place to assign one or more when creating a person.
Departments	Another way of grouping people. See *Group people*, below, for an in-depth comparison of all the various types of groupings.
Password	If the **Person objects provide user passwords** option in the FSD control panel is on, one can log into the Plone site using the **Access Account ID** as a username and the contents of this field as a password.
Personal Assistant(s)	Other people who should have access to edit this person's information (excluding password and the fields under **User Settings**).
Contact Information	
Email	This email address is run through Plone's spam armoring, as yet not widely cracked, before being displayed to visitors. An alternative armoring method ("somebody AT here DOT edu") is available from the FSD control panel under **Site Setup**.
Street Address, City, State, Postal Code, Phone	The required format of the **Office Phone** field, along with its example text, can be set in the FSD control panel—a must for installations outside the United States and Canada.

Professional Information	
Job Titles	As many job titles as you care to provide, one per line. These are all listed on the person's page.
Biography	A rich-text field for the person's biographical information. Since this field can contain all the formatting you can muster—headings, images, and all—it is a wonderful thing to abuse. Fill it with lists of published journal articles, current projects, and anything else appropriate to show on the person's page.
Education	A plain text field where every line represents a conferred degree, certification, or such.
Web Sites	A list of URLs, one per line, to display on the person's page. There is no option to provide link text for these URLs, so you may wish to embed links in the **Biography** field instead.
Committees, Specialties	The committees and specialties to which this person belongs. See the full discussion of FSD's various methods of grouping people under *Group people*, below.
User Settings	
Language, Content Editor	If you leave FSD's user-and-group integration enabled for the Person type, these duplications of the standard Plone options will apply. Integration can be disabled on a type-by-type basis in the FSD control panel under **Site Setup**.

That's a lot of information, but you can fill out only what you'll use. Fields left blank will be omitted from directory pages, labels and all. For more thorough customization, you can write a Faculty/Staff Directory extender product to hide inapplicable fields from your content providers or to collect information that FSD doesn't ordinarily track. See the *Extending Faculty/Staff Directory* chapter for help writing an extender.

Here's how to add people to the directory:

1. From within the directory, pull down the **Add new...** menu, and choose **Person**.
2. Fill out some of the person's attributes. Be sure to assign at least one classification to each person, but don't worry about departments, specialties, or committees yet, as we're about to cover them in detail.

Group people

Most of FSD is geared toward categorizing and correlating people. It provides several different **grouping** types toward this, each with its own abilities and limitations. When you create a new directory, a few groupings are included as examples:

- Three **classifications**: **Faculty**, **Staff**, and **Graduate Students**.
- A **committees folder**. This special type of folder holds **committees**, which in turn represent collaborative groups.
- A **specialties folder**. This special type of folder holds **specialties**, also known as "research interests," with which people can be associated.

A fourth grouping type, not created by default, is the **department**. Like the other types, departments can be added using the **Add new...** menu.

The default groupings can be used as-is or, as is more often done, deleted and replaced with more organization-specific ones. The top-level folders can also be renamed. It is common, for instance, to rename the **Committees** folder as **Workgroups** and the **Specialties** folder as **Research Interests**. (The latter is a particularly good idea, as it increases consistency with the labeling elsewhere in the product.)

People can be assigned to groupings from either of two ends: by editing the grouping itself or by editing the person. (The following screenshots have some options omitted for size.)

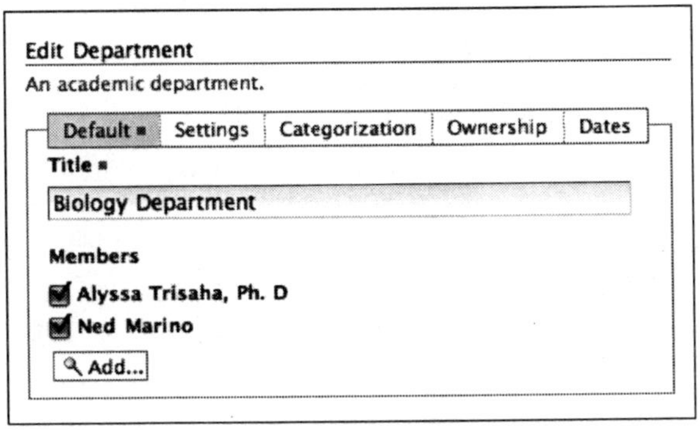

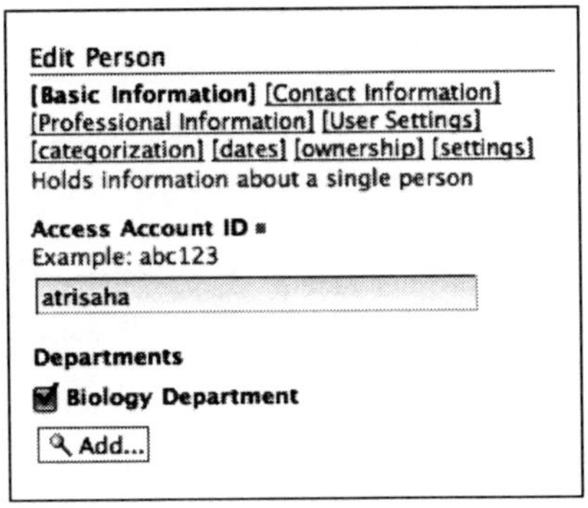

Of people and plants: more general taxonomies with FSD

If your organization doesn't divide neatly into committees, departments, specialties, and classifications, don't panic—you are by no means locked into those categories. While the grouping types have conventional names to make it easy for the majority of academic users to get started, FSD has been stretched as far as to be a catalog of plants rather than people. For example, imagine the Specialties folder renamed to "Taxonomy" and filled with phyla, genera, and species rather than research interests. Add some creative repurposing of fields on the Person type, and you have a serviceable little botany database. You can even write an extender product to relabel the fields; see the next chapter for an example.

All the grouping types collect people, but each has its own additional strengths and weaknesses. Let's examine each in turn and explore some suitable applications.

Classifications

Classifications are the most prominent way of grouping people; all but one of the built-in views have headings for each classification, with lists of people underneath:

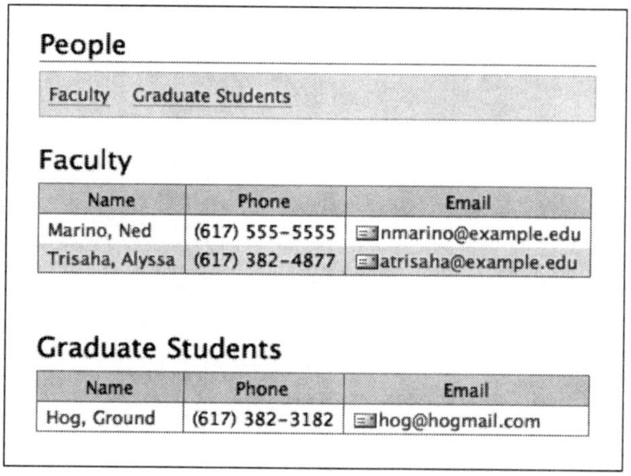

In fact, people lacking a classification won't even show up in these views—a common point of confusion—so be sure to assign at least one to each person.

Committees

Committees' special talent has to do with FSD's user-and-group integration: members of each committee implicitly gain the ability to add and edit items—pages, folders, and so on—within the committee object itself, which acts like a folder. This makes it easy to provide collaboration workspaces without having to teach people how to use the (often confusing) **Sharing** tab.

Specialties

Specialties have two special tricks:

- They can nest inside one another to make a hierarchy.
- When a person is associated with a specialty, a "research topic" can also be provided, describing their specific interest.

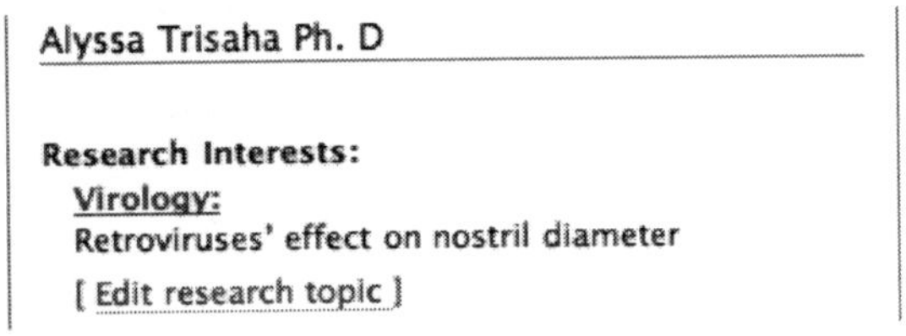

Departments

Departments have a similar trick to that of specialties: their associations can be labeled. For example, a person associated with a department can be dubbed the **Department Head**:

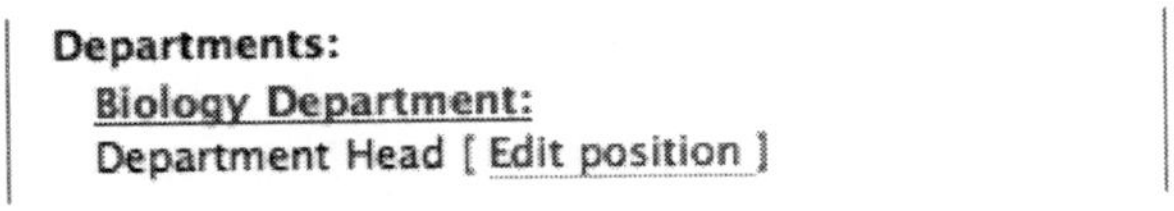

Departments can also exist outside the faculty/staff directory: a big win for many site organizational schemes. What's more, a department can contain committee folders, making it easy to represent, for example, the Budget Committees of different departments.

Avoid the unexpected: stick with one directory.

Though it does little to enforce it, Faculty/Staff Directory encourages the use of only a single directory object per Plone site. This heads off several common pitfalls. For instance, consider a scenario where colleges within a large university are subdivided into departments. If you were to make a separate directory for each college, imagine the trouble when, inevitably, you needed a committee to represent a cross-college collaboration. In which directory would you put it? What about the members of this committee—would you keep two separate copies of them, one in their home college and another in the college housing the collaboration? Real-world scenarios like this abound, and using a single directory up front saves many hard decisions later.

There's also a technical reason to avoid multiple directories. Departments can be placed outside any directory, but, if they are, there is no way to associate them with any particular one. In practice, they will pick one more or less arbitrarily, and they may not always make the choice you expect. Future releases of Faculty/Staff Directory will add proper support for multiple directories for those cases where lists of people really are disjunct, and they will rethink how to represent lists of people outside the directory. See the section *Coming attractions* below for more.

How grouping works: relationships, not containers

Plone's underlying data storage, the ZODB, is a monohierarchy: that is, if Page A is in Folder B, then it cannot also be in Folder C. This presents a challenge for representing membership in FSD groupings by containment. So, while the groupings look and behave like folders in many ways, they do not actually contain people. Instead, membership is modeled using **relationships**, care of the Relations product. Relations keeps a record that "Peggy Smith is *related to* the Budget Committee and the Security Committee", circumventing the one-container limit. Meanwhile, Peggy herself lives in the top level of the faculty/staff directory, along with everyone else. In database lingo, Relations helps FSD act as a miniature relational database—sidestepping ZODB's strict hierarchy.

You, of course, can model your organization's groups without worrying about any of this—except for the following few places where the underpinnings poke through into the user interface:

- If you have the Manager role, you will occasionally see a **Relations** tab while editing within the directory. This is part of Relations' built-in machinery, and you could theoretically use it to manually alter relationships. However, you are more likely to damage internal data structures, so it's best to avoid this and stick to the nicer ways FSD provides. Ordinary users will never see the **Relations** tab, so only site administrators need to watch their steps.

- Since groupings are only *related* to people, no one will show up on their **Contents** tabs. Similarly, it's not possible to add a person to a grouping using the **Add new...** menu, though a future FSD release will include a workaround for the sake of convenience.

Views

FSD provides four views that can be applied to groupings or to the directory itself.

Gallery view

The gallery view shows each person's portrait along with their contact information. Like most of the views, the gallery view groups people under headings representing their classifications, for example Faculty, Staff, or Graduate Students. In practice, gallery view works best for smaller groupings, since its many images make for slow-loading pages. All images are scaled, proportionally, to a single width controllable through the **Edit → Display** tab on the directory.

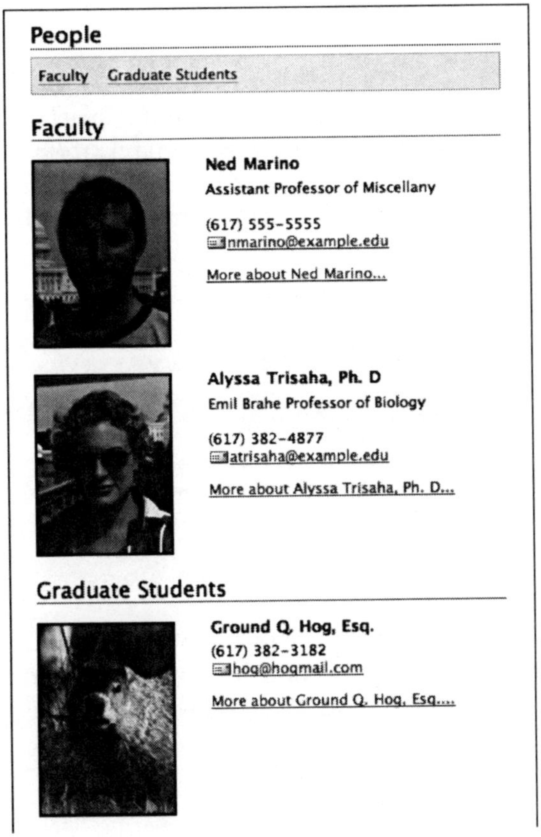

Tabular view

Tabular view is a more selective view, listing only name, phone number, and email—great for larger groupings. Like gallery view, it divides people according to their classification.

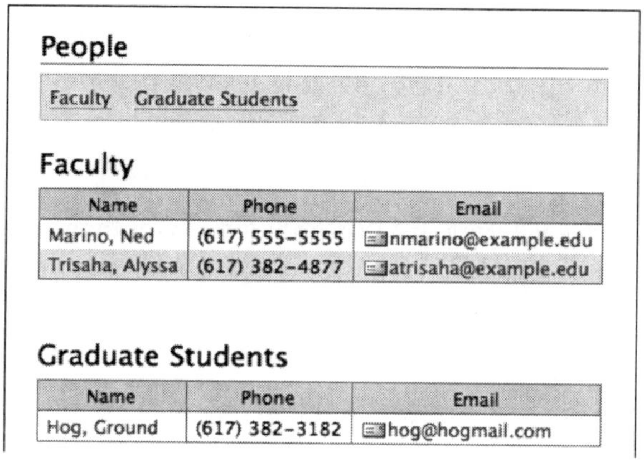

A-Z view

A-Z looks a lot like tabular view on the surface, but it is strictly alphabetical, not splitting people by classification. Its main means of navigation is a linked alphabet at the top of the page, where each letter jumps to the corresponding position in the list. The A-Z view is the best choice when users often need to search by name, without necessarily knowing a person's job function.

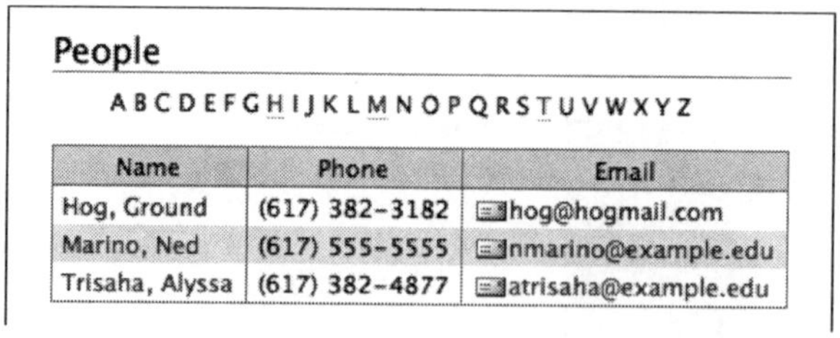

Textual view

Available exclusively on departments, the textual view provides only links to each classification, deferring any listing of people until the user burrows deeper. This is often appropriate for entities of department size, where a full listing of personnel would be unwieldy.

Which views for which types?

Most of the grouping types support only a subset of the four views. As of FSD 2.1.3, they are...

	Gallery	Tabular	A-Z	Textual
Directory	✓	✓	✓	
Classification	✓	✓		
Committee				
Department	✓	✓	✓	✓
Specialty	✓	✓		

Integrate users and groups

One of FSD's most powerful features is the optional integration of its types with Plone's built-in access control facilities. Both people and grouping types are imbued with this user-and-group magic, a huge timesaver to schools that don't already represent these groups in a shared system like LDAP or Active Directory.

Integration begins with the Person type. Any person you create in FSD can act as a normal Plone user: the login name is the person's **Access Account ID**, and the password is the one specified on the person's **Edit** tab. As with a normal user, FSD people can have local roles assigned via the **Sharing** tab or be put into normal Plone groups. In addition, logged-in FSD people automatically get the **Owner** role on their own Person objects, which lets them edit their own biographies and such without having to be manually assigned privileges.

Groupings comprise the other half of the integration story. FSD's groupings act just like normal Plone groups: committees, departments, classifications, and even the directory itself can be searched for and assigned roles on the **Sharing** tab. Give the members of a department access to a departmental intranet, or set up a collaboration area for faculty only—it's all possible without having to tell Plone a second time who belongs in those groups.

Interoperating with enterprise authentication

In the case of fancier setups, with another plugin like PloneLDAP or WebServerAuth handling authentication, FSD needs to be dissuaded from trying to authenticate people using the FSD-managed password: just uncheck the **Person objects provide user passwords** box in the FSD control panel. However, you can still get the advantages of user-and-group integration for **Sharing** tab purposes: after a person authenticates through whatever mechanism you've set up, FSD tries to match up the login name with a person's **Access Account ID**. If a match is found, the logged-in user gets the privileges due the FSD person. (Note that, while logged-in persons are able to edit most of their personal information, they are not allowed to add themselves to groupings like committees, since they would effectively be putting themselves into access-control groups.)

Delegating group administration

Typically in Plone, one needs the Manager role in order to manage groups. This can create a drain on the site administrator's time, since he or she has to be bothered for every addition to or deletion from a group. To help solve this problem, FSD comes with a new role: Personnel Manager. Anyone with that role gets the ability to assign people to departments, specialities, and other types of groupings, as well as to create and edit FSD people. The role can be assigned, like any other, in the **Users and Groups** control panel or locally using the **Sharing** tab.

Coming attractions

In development for over a year, the FSD release code-named "Hateful Haberdasher" represents a major redesign of the product. Its version number may turn out to be 3.0 or 4.0, depending on whether an interstitial infrastructure-focused release, currently under consideration, is made. Planned changes include…

- Proper support for more than a single directory within a site. As a result, departments will no longer need to be able to exist outside a directory; instead, this niche will be served by a full set of FSD views on collections.
- Merging of the grouping types. User feedback has shown that the profusion of slight differences between the types is confusing and arbitrary. The distinction between them will be removed, and the various "special tricks" of each will be applicable on demand.
- Re-implementation of all presentation logic as viewlets. This will let site administrators reorder bits of FSD pages using Plone's **@@manage-viewlets** page. In addition, extenders will be able to add to views without having to customize entire templates.

- A portlet for searching inside faculty/staff directories.
- Many, many under-the-hood improvements which will improve performance, ease future development, and enhance extender products' potential.

Summary

In this chapter, we've explored the capabilities of Faculty/Staff Directory, a flexible product for representing information about people and their organizational relationships. We've seen how to organize people into committees, departments, and classifications and how to represent their research interests. We've also learned how to leverage those groupings for access control and, finally, had an inside look at the future of the product.

If you find that FSD does almost what you want but falls short in some small way, continue on to the next chapter, *Extending Faculty/Staff Directory*.

4
Extending Faculty/Staff Directory

While Faculty/Staff Directory (FSD) collects a great deal of information out of the box—contact and biographical information, group associations, and even rudimentary information about the courses people are teaching—almost every organization needs one or two additional nuggets of data. Experience with many FSD installations has shown that these data are usually specific to one organization—departmental budget numbers or campus IDs—things which wouldn't make sense to add to FSD itself.

However, these special requirements are unarguably important, and FSD recognizes this by providing support for **extenders**, Plone products that expand FSD's capabilities. In this chapter, you will learn how to write a Faculty/Staff Directory extender of your own. The Phrenology Department at the fictitious Plumsberg University will be our example; we'll add two fields to the Person type: a fax number and a list of published papers. We will then see how to use extenders to hide or modify existing fields as well. The extension techniques shown here are applicable, with minor modifications, to all Plone content types, so keep in mind other possible site-specific extensions as we go.

In this tutorial, familiarity with basic Python syntax is handy but not essential. If you run into trouble, the excellent Python tutorial at `http://docs.python.org/tutorial/` will get you up to speed in no time. Don't worry; many Python neophytes have successfully authored extenders without such detailed instruction as in this chapter, so relax and enjoy as we begin with a backstage tour of Faculty/Staff Directory.

A look at Archetypes

All Plone content types—including everything in FSD, like people and departments—are written atop a framework called **Archetypes**, which provides much of their complex behavior:

- The familiar multi-tab **Edit** pages
- Widgets—little snippets of user interface—for displaying and editing various types of fields: dates, simple and styled text, images, so on
- Logic for storing content in and retrieving it from the ZODB or elsewhere

All of this is driven by a **schema**, a data structure that describes a content type field by field. Here, for example, is a snippet of the schema of FSD's **Person** type, defining the **First Name** field:

```
StringField(
    name='firstName',
    widget=StringWidget(
        label=_(u"FacultyStaffDirectory_label_firstName",
default=u"First Name"),
        i18n_domain='FacultyStaffDirectory',
    ),
    required=True,
    schemata="Basic Information",
    searchable=True
),
```

A complete schema is essentially a list of these field definitions.

Because practically all of a type's behavior depends on its schema, a lot of customization power is available by tweaking it. Historically, this has been done by subclassing: creating new types that inherit all the features of the old and adding some new ones. However, this approach is fraught with limitations:

- Existing content of the old type can't take advantage of the new features
- Pieces of content that talk about the old type—like collections that search for items by type—don't see the new type
- Existing bits of code, like catalog queries that fetch items by type, remain stuck in the past

Of course, these properties might be desirable depending on your use case, but in ours, they're just a nuisance:

- We have no need to keep two types of person around; we simply want to give the one and only representation more functionality
- We may have existing Persons, which need the new features, and would rather not have to recreate them as a new type
- We have the existing-code problem in spades: FSD's types reference each other by name, making it impossible to subclass one type without doing them all

Thus, instead of making a new type, we'd much rather extend the existing one in place. Fortunately, extending Archetypes schemas is the bread and butter of an easy-to-use framework called, aptly, `archetypes.schemaextender`.

Introducing schemaextender

Starting in Plone 3, Archetypes provides an opportunity for third-party code to modify schemas on the fly. It exposes a point of **adaptation** here, in `BaseObject`, one of the most foundational subclasses of every content type:

```
1  class BaseObject(Referenceable):
2      # (some code omitted here)
3
4      def Schema(self):
5          """Return a (wrapped) schema instance
6          for this object instance.
7          """
8          schema = ISchema(self)
9          return ImplicitAcquisitionWrapper(schema, self)
```

Line 8 is where the magic happens. This line has always determined the schema, but the `ISchema` adapter lookup—which essentially says "Find me the preferred chunk of code that knows how to compute schemas."—is new. We'll discuss adaptation itself shortly, but the upshot is that third-party code has the opportunity to plug in its own ways of determining schemas—in our case, to say "Insert a few new fields here."

Without further clever tricks, there's only room for one piece of code to plug in a schema-determiner for a given object. `archetypes.schemaextender` steps in to act as a clearinghouse, allowing more than one to coexist. It also provides a few other ribs on which to hang the flesh of extenders, helping to keep them short and well structured.

Start your extender

There are several competing ways to start on a new extender:

- A free Java application called ArgoUML lets you draw out your extensions as a UML diagram, which you run through a code generator, ArchGenXML, to create your actual product. However, ArgoUML is notoriously buggy and confusing to use, and the simplicity of most extenders makes it a bad trade-off.
- The ZopeSkel templates for the `paster` code generator, which we will use in the *Going Live* and *Styling Your Site* chapters, include one for making Archetypes types. Rather than taking a UML file as input, `paster` asks a series of questions via the command line and then lays out the skeleton of a product. It then provides a command-line interface for adding functionality. A future version of FSD will include a template for making FSD extenders using this process. At the moment, however, there remain some kinks to work out; the version in development works, but it yields a somewhat complex result that is difficult to learn from.
- Copying an existing product and making changes. FSD 2.1.3 ships with a simple example extender, which adds a **Mobile Phone** field to the Person type. Because it is concise enough to understand completely and simple to adapt to our needs, this is the route we'll take in this chapter.

Copy MobilePhoneExtender

Here is an overview of how we'll begin:

1. Make a copy of the sample extender, MobilePhoneExtender.
2. Rename some of its folders so it's no longer called MobilePhoneExtender.
3. Replace some references to the name MobilePhoneExtender in its code so it continues to work.

Our first two orders of business are to make a copy of MobilePhoneExtender and give it a new name:

1. Find your copy of Faculty/Staff Directory. If you are using buildout's default settings, it's probably in your buildout folder within the `eggs` folder, named `Products.FacultyStaffDirectory-2.1.3-py2.4.egg`. The version numbers at the end may differ slightly.
2. Once you have found the FacultyStaffDirectory egg, find the example extender inside it. For example, in version 2.1.3, it is at **Products.FacultyStaffDirectory-2.1.3-py2.4.egg → Products → FacultyStaffDirectory → examples → Products.MobilePhoneExtender**.

3. Make a copy of `Products.MobilePhoneExtender`, and place the copy into the `src` folder of your buildout.

   Now that we have duplicated the example extender, we can rename two of its folders to make it our own:

4. Rename `Products.MobilePhoneExtender` to `Products.PlumsbergPhrenologyExtender`. This name is a good choice for the following reasons:
   - It encompasses what the product does now (or will do once we finish this tutorial) and what it is likely to do in the future. "Products.PlumsbergFaxAndPublishedPapersExtender" would be more informative, but it would also become misleading if we decided to add more fields later, and renaming a product makes buildout, PyPI, and Zope itself throw fits of varying seriousness. (Of course, if you are building a generally-useful extender for public consumption, you should forgo naming it after your institution or department and choose a name that reflects its functionality. This tutorial assumes an extender meant for in-house use.)
   - Using a **namespace** of **Products** gets us some functionality for free. First, it gives us the option of installing our extender simply by dragging its inner `MobilePhoneExtender` folder into a Plone installation's `products` folder. Second, it saves a step when installing it using buildout: we need add it under only `eggs`, not under the `zcml` section as well. (This requirement evaporates in Plone 3.3, but this extender will happily run on existing sites all the way back to Plone 2.5.)

5. Inside **Products.MobilePhoneExtender → Products**, rename the **MobilePhoneExtender** folder to **PlumsbergPhrenologyExtender**. Technically, there's no need for the name of the egg (`Products.PlumsbergPhrenologyExtender`) and the name of the inner package (`PlumsbergPhrenologyExtender`) to match, but experience has shown that it causes confusion when they don't. For that reason, most Plone products follow this convention.

Finally, we'll need to update several pieces of code in the product that refer to `Products.MobilePhoneExtender` by name. If you don't already have a good multi-file search-and-replace tool, this is an excellent time to get one. Here are a few suggestions for some common platforms:

Mac	TextWrangler is a free version of BBEdit, missing mostly the costlier product's HTML editing facilities and version control integration. However, its multi-file find-and-replace are the best on the platform. TextMate is another fine choice; it has a healthy plugin ecosystem and includes Subversion integration as well. Though commercial software, it has a 30-day free trial. It costs $59 U.S. at the time of this writing, and there is an additional 15% discount for students, faculty, and educational staff.
Windows	E is a Windows-native takeoff of TextMate. jEdit is a well-supported free alternative.
Linux/UNIX	If you're a command-line jockey, you can feel free to use sed. We also certainly won't try to pry anyone away from vi or Emacs. For those just getting started, jEdit runs great on Linux and has a relatively approachable interface.

6. With your search-and-replace tool of choice, search all the files within `Products.PlumsbergPhrenologyExtender`, and replace all occurrences of "MobilePhoneExtender" with "PlumsbergPhrenologyExtender". If you've accumulated any `.pyc` files, feel free to skip those; those are just temporary files left over by the Python compiler and will be automatically regenerated the next time the corresponding modules are loaded.

To double-check, these are the files where you should find occurrences of "MobilePhoneExtender" to replace:

- `__init.py__`
- `Install.py`
- `person.py`
- `skins.xml` (in `profiles` → `default`)
- `skins.xml` (in `profiles` → `uninstall`)
- `README.txt` (though this doesn't affect functionality and should be rewritten to reflect your product)
- `setup.py`

Test your work so far

To make certain we have a solid starting point, let's fire up Plone and make sure our new extender still works. We haven't yet done anything but rename it, so it should still add a **Mobile Phone** field to Person.

1. Start a fresh buildout using `paster`:

```
paster create -t plone3_buildout phrenology_extender_buildout

Selected and implied templates:
  ZopeSkel#plone3_buildout  A buildout for Plone 3 projects

Variables:
  egg:      phrenology_extender_buildout
  package:  phrenology_extender_buildout
  project:  phrenology_extender_buildout
Enter plone_version (Which Plone version to install) ['3.2.1']:
Enter zope2_install (Path to Zope 2 installation; leave blank to fetch one) ['']:
Enter plone_products_install (Path to directory containing Plone products; leave blank to fetch one) ['']:
Enter zope_user (Zope root admin user) ['admin']:
Enter zope_password (Zope root admin password) ['']: admin
Enter http_port (HTTP port) [8080]:
Enter debug_mode (Should debug mode be "on" or "off"?) ['off']:
Enter verbose_security (Should verbose security be "on" or "off"?) ['off']:
Creating template plone3_buildout
[...Gory details omitted...]
-----------------------------------------------------------
Generation finished
You probably want to run python bootstrap.py and then edit
buildout.cfg before running bin/buildout -v

See README.txt for details
-----------------------------------------------------------
```

2. As `paster` says, run `bootstrap.py` using the copy of Python you use to run Plone:

   ```
   cd phrenology_extender_buildout
   python2.4 bootstrap.py
   ```

   An invaluable tool for egg development is `eggtractor`, a **buildout extension** that automatically loads anything you put into the `src` folder. Since our egg is already there, we can cause it to load by adding `eggtractor` to our buildout configuration and running buildout:

3. In `phrenology_extender_buildout` → `buildout.cfg` under the `[buildout]` section, add `eggtractor` to the `extensions` parameter:

   ```
   [buildout]
   extensions = buildout.eggtractor
   ```

4. Run buildout to download and install the packages our egg depends on: namely, `archetypes.schemaextender` and Faculty/Staff Directory itself. From within the `phrenology_extender_buildout` folder...

   ```
   bin/buildout
   ```

   Finally, start up Zope, and manually confirm that PlumsbergPhrenologyExtender still adds its **Mobile Phone** field properly:

5. Start up Zope.

   ```
   bin/instance fg
   ```

6. Do any error messages appear on the command line? If so, they probably point to a mistake made during the find and replace. For example, an error message like this…

   ```
     File "/Users/erikrose/Zope/phrenology_extender_buildout/
   src/Products.PlumsbergPhrenologyExtender/Products/
   PlumsbergPhrenologyExtender/__init__.py", line 6, in ?
       from Products.MobilePhoneExtender.person import PersonExtender
   ImportError: No module named MobilePhoneExtender.person
   ```

…complains that we missed a spot in `PlumsbergPhrenologyExtender` → `__init__.py`—on line 6, specifically. Head over to `__init__.py` in your text editor, and rub out that spurious remnant of "MobilePhoneExtender." If you need to find line 107, don't wear out your arrow key counting by hand. All the text editors recommended above have either a jump-to-numbered-line command or the ability to show line numbers. Failing that, the error message should include the problem line: use the Find command to track it down.

7. Visit `http://127.0.0.1:8080/manage` in a browser.
8. Create a new Plone site.
9. Install Faculty/Staff Directory and PlumsbergPhrenologyExtender using the **Add-on Products** control panel.
10. Create a new Faculty/Staff Directory object at the root of your Plone site.
11. Add a Person.
12. While editing the new Person, there should be a **Mobile Phone** field on its **Contact Information** page.

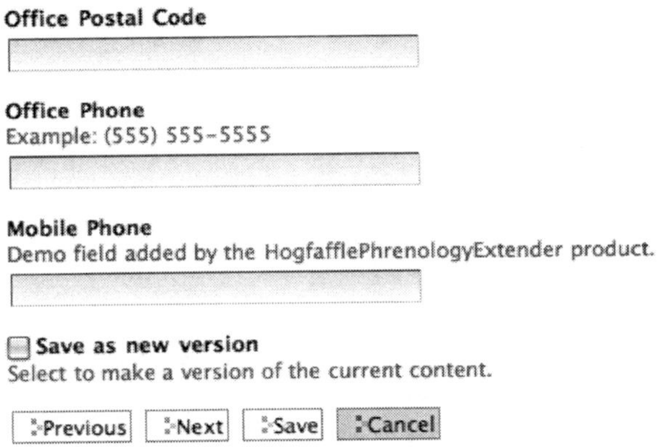

If you go back to the **Add-on Products** control panel and uninstall PlumsbergPhrenologyExtender, does the **Mobile Phone** field go away? If so, everything is working fine; move on to the next section. If not, double-check your find-and-replace results. Getting everything working before moving on will minimize frustration and wasted time in the long run.

Adapters: the anatomy of an Extender

The guts of the sample extender live in `person.py`, found in `Products.PlumsbergPhrenologyExtender` → `Products` → `PlumsbergPhrenologyExtender` → `person.py`. The operative part, following a few rather dry imports and minor declarations, is the `PersonExtender` class, just 25 lines long:

```
class PersonExtender(object):
    """Adapter that adds a Mobile Phone field to Person.

    You could also change or delete existing fields (though you
        might violate assumptions made in other code). To do that,
        implement ISchemaModifier instead of ISchemaExtender.
    """
    adapts(IPerson)
    implements(ISchemaExtender)

    _fields = [
            _StringExtensionField('mobilePhone',
                required=False,
                searchable=True,
                schemata="Contact Information",
                widget=StringWidget(
                    label=u"Mobile Phone",
                    description=u"Demo field added by the
                      MobilePhoneExtender product.",
                )
            )
        ]

    def __init__(self, context):
        self.context = context

    def getFields(self):
        return self._fields
```

Let's examine how it works so we can understand the modifications we're about to make.

Take this, make that

A schema extender is an **adapter**, a sort of translation layer that takes one kind of object and delivers another.

> **Why adapters?**
>
> Relatively new in Plone's bag of tricks, adapters were introduced as a substitute for earlier techniques, which had grown too unwieldy—in particular, extremely deep class hierarchies, which ironically limited code reuse. Because a typical Plone class referred, directly or indirectly, to dozens of other classes by name, it inherited the assumptions of all of them. It was thus very difficult to use any class outside of Plone without bringing half of Plone with it. Classes couldn't be easily repurposed even within Plone, being so tightly coupled to so many assumptions. Finally, testing was a challenge, requiring elaborate setup to meet the requirements of such heavyweight classes.
>
> Component-based programming, of which adapters are a manifestation, loosens this coupling. Notice that `PersonExtender` subclasses only Python's built-in `object` class. Instead of being bound to the `Person` class by name, it refers to it by interface, `IPerson`. This means an alternative implementation of `Person`—in a test harness, for example—could be provided without also bringing in every one of its superclasses. Adapters make code harder to reason about by looking at it—one has to track down which class it's talking about when it says `IPerson`—but it opens up a lot of code to reuse.

`PersonExtender` is an adapter that takes a Person object and yields something that can produce a list of fields to add. Lines 6 and 7 spell out this claim so Plone's adapter machinery knows when to activate it. First let's examine line 6:

```
6       adapts(IPerson)
```

This line means "Take effect for any object that implements the `IPerson` interface—that is, that claims to act like an FSD person." Discriminating by interface rather than class name is overkill much of the time, but it leaves the door open for someone to make an alternative implementation of Person—and our extender would still work. We won't need to change the `adapts` lines for PlumsbergPhrenologyExtender since, like the mobile phone example, it adds fields to Person. However, if you wanted to extend a different type, here are the interfaces to substitute for `IPerson`. You would also need to change the `import` statement a few lines above.

Type	**Interface**	**Add this import to the top of the file.**
`Classification`	`IClassification`	`from Products.FacultyStaffDirectory.interfaces.classification import IClassification`
`Committee`	`ICommittee`	`from Products.FacultyStaffDirectory.interfaces.Committee import ICommittee`
`CommitteeMembership`	`ICommitteeMembership`	`from Products.FacultyStaffDirectory.interfaces.CommitteeMembership import ICommitteeMembership`
`CommitteesFolder`	`ICommitteesFolder`	`from Products.FacultyStaffDirectory.interfaces.CommitteesFolder import ICommitteesFolder`
`Course`	`ICourse`	`from Products.FacultyStaffDirectory.interfaces.Course import ICourse`
`Department`	`IDepartment`	`from Products.FacultyStaffDirectory.interfaces.Department import IDepartment`

Type	Interface	Add this import to the top of the file.
`DepartmentalMembership`	`IDepartmentalMembership`	`from Products.FacultyStaffDirectory.interfaces.DepartmentalMembership import IDepartmentalMembership`
`FacultyStaffDirectory`	`IFacultyStaffDirectory`	`from Products.FacultyStaffDirectory.interfaces.FacultyStaffDirectory import IFacultyStaffDirectory`
`Person`	`IPerson`	`from Products.FacultyStaffDirectory.interfaces.Person import IPerson`
`SpecialtiesFolder`	`ISpecialtiesFolder`	`from Products.FacultyStaffDirectory.interfaces.SpecialtiesFolder import ISpecialtiesFolder`
`Specialty`	`ISpecialty`	`from Products.FacultyStaffDirectory.interfaces.Specialty import ISpecialty`
`SpecialtyInformation`	`ISpecialtyInformation`	`from Products.FacultyStaffDirectory.interfaces.SpecialtyInformation import ISpecialtyInformation`

Now that we've decided what to adapt *from*, let's see what to adapt *to*:

```
7       implements(ISchemaExtender)
```

This line declares that PersonExtender adapts Person *to* an `ISchemaExtender`: that is, to something that can return a list of fields to be added to an object. (For the curious, detailed documentation of the `ISchemaExtender` interface can be found in `archetypes.schemaextender`'s `interfaces.py`.)

Constructor boilerplate

Before adding our fields, we must conform to a convention required of all adapters. When an adapter is instantiated by the underlying framework, its `__init__` method (called the **constructor**) is passed the object being adapted: in our case, a Person. However, we're not really interested in which Person it is; we do exactly the same thing in any case. Thus, we declare a constructor that takes the passed-in Person, stores it away in a member variable, and then forgets about it:

```
    def __init__(self, context):
        self.context = context
```

These lines can be left as-is in almost all extenders. (Note that `context` here is unrelated to the same term used in acquisition—a common point of confusion.)

Our claims of functionality made and convention satisfied, we can at last move on to adding fields.

Add the fax and publications fields

Besides the constructor above, a schema extender really requires only one function: `getFields`, which returns a list of fields to add.

```
    def getFields(self):
        return self._fields
```

The list of fields doesn't live within the `getFields` method; it comes instead from the `_fields` attribute of the class. We could have written `getFields` like this...

```
def getFields(self):
    return [
        _StringExtensionField('mobilePhone',
            required=False,
            searchable=True,
            schemata="Contact Information",
            widget=StringWidget(
                label=u"Mobile Phone",
                description=u"Demo field added by the
  MobilePhoneExtender product.",
            )
        )
    ]
```

...and it would have worked, but it would also have been deathly slow, as it would require the expensive construction of a `_StringExtensionField` each time the schema is computed—which is over 70 times for a default edit page in Plone 3.

To improve speed, we make our list of fields once and sock it away in the `_fields` attribute for later:

```
9       _fields = [
10              _StringExtensionField('mobilePhone',
11                  required=False,
12                  searchable=True,
13                  schemata="Contact Information",
14                  widget=StringWidget(
15                      label=u"Mobile Phone",
16                      description=u"Demo field added by the
  MobilePhoneExtender product.",
17                  )
18              )
19          ]
```

It is in `_fields` that we make the bulk of our customizations.

1. The fax number we introduce is patterned after the sample `mobilePhone` field. Substitute the following for the similar code on lines 10-18 above:

```
_StringExtensionField('fax',
    required=False,
    searchable=True,
    schemata="Contact Information",
    widget=StringWidget(
        label=u"Fax",
        description=u"Example: (555) 555-5555",
    )
)
```

The changes are...

- The field name and label. Label and details can change in the future, but the field name, 'fax', must remain the same once you begin storing data in the field.
- The description, which we made more useful. In your own extenders, the entire description line can be deleted if it isn't needed.

If you are already familiar with Archetypes programming, you might notice that our field types are a bit unfamiliar: where you might expect to see a `StringField` for a single-line text field, we use a `_StringExtensionField`. This is a peculiarity of the schemaextender framework: any field added by an extender must subclass `ExtensionField`. Our copy of `person.py` does this for `StringField` already:

```
class _StringExtensionField(ExtensionField, StringField):
    pass
```

We can follow this pattern for other types of fields as well. For example, to use a `TextField` to store a styled list of publications, we declare a `_TextExtensionField`.

1. Make a `_TextExtensionField` class that inherits from both `ExtensionField` and `TextField`. Our two `ExtensionFields` should look like this:

```
class _StringExtensionField(ExtensionField, StringField):
    pass

class _TextExtensionField(ExtensionField, TextField):
    pass
```

Next, we add our publication list field.

2. Add a **Selected Publications** field to the `_fields` list. `_fields` should now look like this:

```
_fields = [
        _StringExtensionField('fax',
            required=False,
            searchable=True,
            schemata="Contact Information",
            widget=StringWidget(
                label=u"Fax"
            )
        ),
        _TextExtensionField(
            name='publications',
            allowable_content_types=('text/html', 'application/
msword'),
            widget=RichWidget(
                label=u'Selected Publications',
                description=u"References to select publications
you would like to feature on your directory page"
            ),
            schemata="Professional Information",
            searchable=True,
            validators=('isTidyHtmlWithCleanup',),
            default_output_type='text/x-html-safe'
        )
    ]
```

Deconstructing the above...

`_TextExtensionField`	Our extender-compatible version of `TextField`, which provides a place to store multi-line text or HTML. If you are working on your second extender, you might want to take a look at the many other types of fields that are available as well: dates, numbers of various sorts, uploaded images, menus, and many more. The built-in ones are documented at `http://plone.org/documentation/manual/plone-core-developer-reference/specific-areas/content-types/fields/fields-reference/`, and even more are available as third-party products. DataGridField, which provides arbitrarily typed columnar input with a polished, client-side UI, is especially worth a look.
`allowable_content_types`	A list (a tuple, technically) of MIME types, which determine what choices of input format the user will have.
`widget=RichWidget`	Chooses a multi-line formatted editor rather than the plain box the default, `StringWidget`, provides. More widgets are documented at `http://plone.org/documentation/manual/plone-core-developer-reference/specific-areas/content-types/fields/widgets-reference/`
`schemata`	Controls which tab each field appears on during editing.
`validators`	`isTidyHtmlWithCleanup` is the name of a **validator**, a routine that runs after the edit form is submitted and makes sure the input is acceptable. This one has the side effect of sprucing up the input HTML. See `http://plone.org/documentation/manual/archetypes-developer-manual/fields/validator-reference` for many more validators you can use.

At this point, our new fields should show up—at least on the **Edit** tab. Save your work, start up (or restart) Zope, install our extender if necessary, and check the **Contact Information** and **Professional Information** tabs within a Person's **Edit** tab.

Once you troubleshoot the inevitable punctuation mistakes (remember, the bottom line of a traceback is the bottom line—it almost always points out the location of the error), we can move on to the last piece of extender construction.

Show the new fields in views

The last order of business is to make **Fax** and **Publications** show up on person pages. They're initially hidden because FSD ships with a rather involved custom template for viewing Persons: in nicely arranging everything on the page, it explicitly names the fields to show, and it's not aware of our new ones. Thus, we need to manually insert our fields into the `person_view` template.

Fortunately, the sample extender comes with a copy of `person_view` already installed; all we have to do is make some additions. Take a deep breath, dive down to `Products.PlumsbergPhrenologyExtender` → `Products` → `PlumsbergPhrenologyExtender` → `skins` → `PlumsbergPhrenologyExtender` → `person_view.pt` in your text editor, and we'll make our last change.

1. Search `person_view.pt` for the word "mobile". You should turn up a short section like this:

   ```
   <div tal:define="mobilePhone python:context.get('mobilePhone')"
   tal:condition="mobilePhone" class="tel officePhone">
      <span class="type">Mobile</span>:
      <span class="value" tal:content="mobilePhone">[mobile phone
   number]</span>
   </div>
   ```

These somewhat HTML-ish lines use Plone's templating language, TAL. In case you're not familiar with it and want to understand what we're about to change, a great TAL reference is `http://docs.zope.org/zope2/zope2book/AppendixC.html`.

2. Replace all occurrences of `mobilePhone` in the above with `fax`.
3. Replace the `Mobile` label with `Fax` as well.

The only difference here from a typical Archetypes template is the accessor: `get('mobilePhone')`. More often in Archetypes, one sees `getMobilePhone()`, but extender fields don't get dedicated accessors, so we need to use the former syntax.

4. Find a good place to insert the **Publications** field, such as after this **Biography** div:

   ```
   <div tal:condition="here/getBiography" class="biography">
       <h3 i18n:translate="FacultyStaffDirectory_label_
     biography">Biography:</h3>
       <span tal:content="structure context/getBiography" />
   </div>
   ```

5. Insert this after the above:

```
 <div tal:define="publications python:context.get('publications')"
class="biography" tal:condition="publications">
    <h3>Selected Publications:</h3>
    <span tal:content="structure publications" />
</div>
```

And presto—our two new fields show up on person pages!

We now have a complete Faculty/Staff Directory extender product. If you would like your extender to instead (or also) rename, change, or hide fields, continue on to the next section.

Hide or change existing fields

Extenders aren't limited to just adding fields. Sometimes it can be useful to relabel, hide, or otherwise change Faculty/Staff Directory's stock fields. In those cases, we change the interface to which we're adapting. Rather than `ISchemaExtender`, which adds fields, we implement `ISchemaModifier`, which modifies them. The adapter declaration changes from this...

```
implements(ISchemaExtender)
```

...to this...

```
implements(ISchemaModifier)
```

When changing fields, be cautious. If you violate assumptions made in other code, it could result in errors. For example, changing a numerical field to a text field would be risky, but hiding an unrequired field should be safe, since, as far as dependent code is concerned, it's just as if the user left the field blank.

> Part of the `ISchemaModifier` contract actually requires implementors to take an oath before using it. Raise your right hand, and repeat the following: "I hereby do solemnly swear to refrain, under all circumstances, from using this adapter for Evil. I will not delete fields, change field types, or do other breakable and evil things."

Let's make, as an example, an extender that hides one field and renames another. We'll hide **Web Sites**—which shouldn't cause problems, since it's not a required field—and rename the **Image** field to **Personal Photo**. Here is the complete contents of `person.py` for an extender that implements this. The rest of the product remains unchanged from the previous example, except that you don't need any changes to the `person_view` template.

```
from archetypes.schemaextender.interfaces import ISchemaModifier
from zope.interface import implements
from zope.component import adapts

from Products.FacultyStaffDirectory.interfaces.person import IPerson


class PersonExtender(object):
    """Schema modifier that hides the Web Sites field and renames the
     Image field."""

    adapts(IPerson)
    implements(ISchemaModifier)

    def __init__(self, context):
        self.context = context

    def fiddle(self, schema):
        """Replace the Web Sites field with a copy that's hidden, and
   replace the Image field with a copy that's renamed."""

        # Hide the Web Sites field:
        new_field = schema['websites'].copy()
        new_field.widget.visible = {'edit': 'invisible', 'view':
          'invisible'}
        schema['websites'] = new_field

        # Rename the Images field:
        new_field = schema['image'].copy()
        new_field.widget.label = 'Personal Photo'
        schema['image'] = new_field
```

The `fiddle` method is the workhorse of the extender, taking the place of `getFields` from our earlier example. It consists of two groups of three lines, each of which follows the same pattern:

1. Make a copy of the stock field, and store it in the variable `new_field`. In accordance with the `ISchemaModifier` documentation (in `archetypes.schemaextender`'s `interfaces.py`), we must make a copy of each field before modifying it. Otherwise, our changes will leak into other Plone sites within the Zope instance, because the Person schema is shared across them.

   ```
   new_field = schema['image'].copy()
   ```

2. Make changes to the copy of the field.

   ```
   new_field.widget.label = 'Personal Photo'
   ```

3. Attach the copy to the schema in place of the original.

   ```
   schema['image'] = new_field
   ```

The `fiddle` method, as you can see, modifies the schema in place and doesn't return anything. As long as you make the requisite copy of each field, you can change whatever you like: labels, descriptions, widgets—anything that doesn't create surprises for code that uses the field's contents.

Off-the-shelf extenders

Though the majority of extenders address organization-specific needs, this isn't necessarily the case. Some extenders reach beyond the walls of their birth organizations and provide generally useful functionality. For example, `fsd.cmfbibliographyat` is a simple integration of a complex bibliography product into FSD: `http://pypi.python.org/pypi/fsd.cmfbibliographyat`. Other extenders may be available at the Python Package Index (`http://pypi.python.org/pypi/`); just search for "facultystaffdirectory".

Summary

Congratulations! You've have built an example extender product and learned enough about the underlying framework to go back and revise it for your own institution's needs. You have seen…

- How the Archetypes framework fits within Plone
- The basic concepts of using adapters in Plone's component architecture
- How to add fields to any FSD content type
- How to change or hide fields that don't fit your requirements

5
Blogs and Forums

Blogs and forums have much to offer in a school setting. They help faculty and students communicate despite large class sizes. They engage students in conversations with each other. And they provide an easy way for instructors and staff members to build their personal reputations—and, thereby, the reputation of your institution. In this chapter, we consider how best to build blogs and forums in Plone. Along the way, we cite education-domain examples and point out tips for keeping your site stable and your users smiling.

Plone's blogging potential

Though Plone wasn't conceived as a blogging platform, its role as a full-fledged content management system gives it all the functionality of a blog and more. With a few well-placed tweaks, it can present an interface that puts users of other blogging packages right at home while letting you easily maintain ties between your blogs and the rest of your site.

Generally speaking, blog entries are…

- Prominently labeled by date and organized in reverse chronological order
- Tagged by subject
- Followed by reader comments
- Syndicated using RSS or other protocols

Plone provides all of these, with varying degrees of polish, out of the box:

- News items make good blog entries, and the built-in News portlet lists the most recent few, in reverse chronological order and with publication dates prominently shown. A more comprehensive, paginated list can easily be made using collections.

- Categories are a basic implementation of tags.
- Plone's built-in commenting can work on any content type, News Items included.
- Every collection has its own RSS feed.

Add-on products: free as in puppies

In addition to Plone's built-in tools, this chapter will explore the capabilities of several third-party add-ons. Open-source software is often called "free as in beer" or "free as in freedom". As typical of Plone add-ons, the products we will consider are both. However, they are also "free as in puppies".

Who can resist puppies? They are heart-meltingly cute and loads of fun, but it's easy to forget, when their wet little noses are in your face, that they come with responsibility. Likewise, add-ons are free to install and use, but they also bring hidden costs:

- Products can hold you back. If you depend on one that doesn't support a new version of Plone, you'll face a choice between the product and the Plone upgrade. This situation is most likely at major version boundaries: for example, upgrading from Plone 3.x to Plone 4. Minor upgrades, as from Plone 3.2 to 3.3, should be fairly uneventful. (This was not always true with Plone 2.x, but release numbering has since gotten a dose of sanity.)
- One place products often fall short is uninstallation. It takes care to craft a quality uninstallation routine; low-quality or prerelease products sometimes fail to uninstall cleanly, leaving bits of themselves scattered throughout your site. They can even prevent your site from displaying any pages at all (often due to leaving remnants in `portal_actions`), and you may have to repair things by hand through the ZMI or, failing that, through an afternoon of fun with the Python debugger. The moral: even trying a product can be a risk. Test installation and uninstallation on a copy of your site before committing to one, and back up your `Data.fs` file before installing or uninstalling on production servers. The *Maintenance, Backups, and Upgrades* chapter shows you how.
- Pace of work varies widely. Reporting a bug against an actively developed product might get you a new release within the week. Hitting a bug in an abandoned one could leave you fixing it yourself or paying someone else to. (Fortunately, there are scads of Plone consultants for hire in the `#plone` IRC channel and on the `plone-users` mailing list.)

- In addition to the above, products that add new content types (like blog entries, for instance) bring a risk of lock-in proportional to the amount of content you create with them. If a product is abandoned by its maintainer or you decide to stop using it for some other reason, you will need to migrate its content into some other type, either by writing custom scripts or by copying and pasting.

These considerations are major drivers of this chapter's recommendations. For each of the top three Plone blogging strategies, we'll outline its capabilities, tick off its pros and cons, and estimate how high-maintenance a puppy it will be. Remember, even though puppies can be some work, a well-chosen and well-trained one becomes a best friend for life.

News Items: blogging for the hurried or risk-averse

Using news items as blog entries is, in true Extreme Programming style, "the simplest thing that could possibly work". Nonetheless, it's a surprisingly flexible practice and will disappoint only if you need features like pings, trackbacks, and remote editor integration. Here is an example front page of a Plone blog built using only news items, collections, and the built-in portlets:

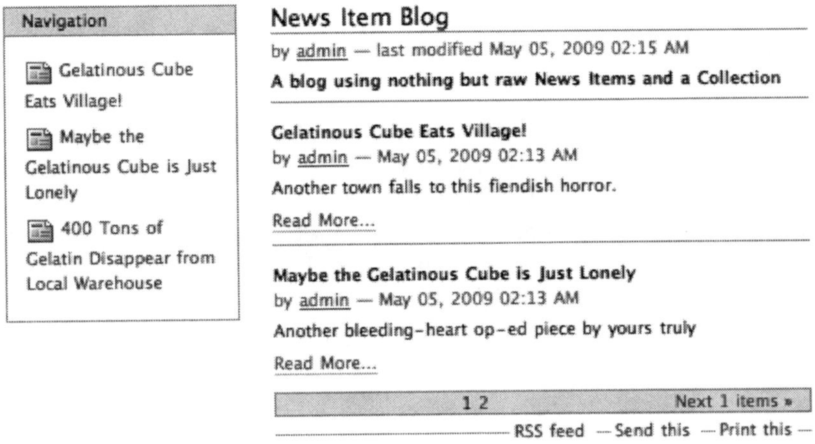

Structure of a news-item blog

A blog in Plone can be as simple as a folder full of News Items, further organized into subfolders if necessary. Add a collection showing the most recent News Items to the top-level folder, and set it as its default page. As illustrated below, use an **Item Type** criterion for the collection to pull in the News Items, and use a **Location** criterion to exclude those created outside the blog folder:

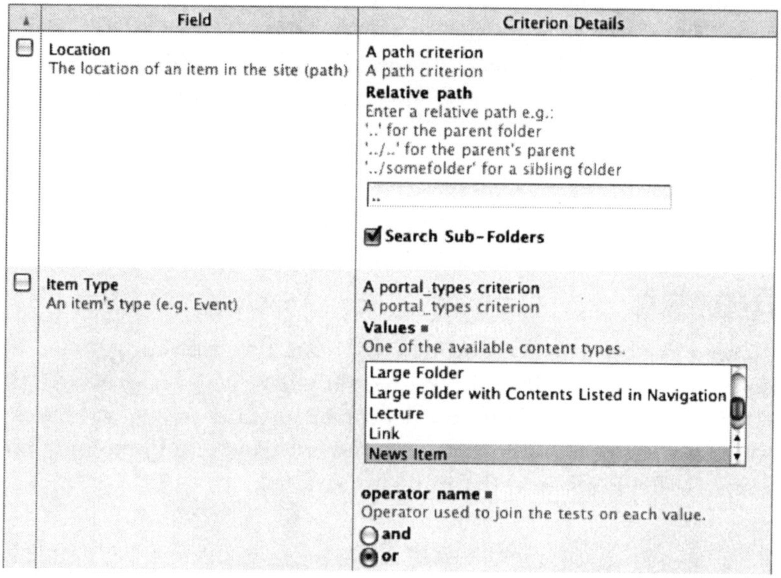

To provide pagination—recommended once the length of listings starts to noticeably impact download or render timetime—use the **Limit Search Results** option on the collection. One inconsistency is that only the Summary and Tabular Views on collections support pagination; Standard View (which shows the same information) does not. This means that Summary View, which sports a **Read more** link and is a bit more familiar to most blog users, is typically a good choice.

Go easy on the pagination

More items displayed per page is better. User tests on prototypes of `gap.com`'s online store have suggested that, at least when selling shirts, more get sold when all are on one big page. Perhaps it's because users are faced with a louder mental "Continue or leave?" when they reach the end of a page. Regardless, it's something to consider when setting page size using a collection's **Number of Items** setting; you may want to try several different numbers and see how it affects the frequency with which your listing pages show up as "exit pages" in a web analytics package like AWStats.

As a starting point, 50 is a sane choice, assuming your listings show only the title and description of each entry (as the built-in views do). The ideal number will be a trade-off between tempting visitors to leave with page breaks and keeping load and render times tolerable.

Finally, make sure to sort the entries by publication date. Set this up on the front-page collection's **Criteria** tab by selecting **Effective Date** and reversing the display order:

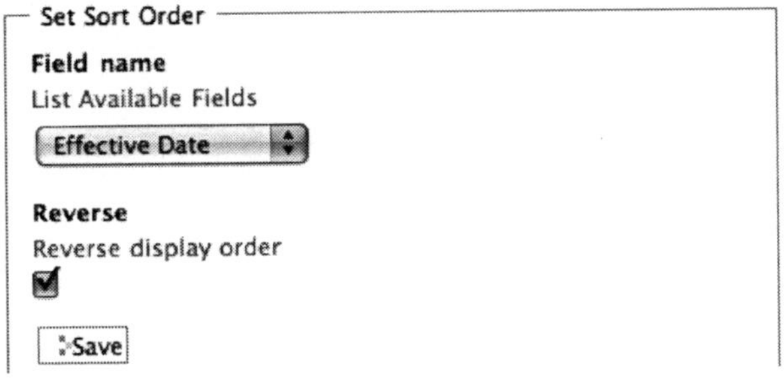

As with all solutions in this chapter, a blog built on raw **News Items** can easily handle either single- or multi-author scenarios; just assign rights appropriately on the **Sharing** tab of the blog folder.

News Item pros and cons

Unadorned News Items are a great way to get started fast and confer practically zero upgrade risk, since they are maintained as part of Plone itself. However, be aware of these pointy edges you might bang into when using them as blog entries:

- With the built-in views, logged-out users can't see the authors or the publication dates of entries. Even logged-in users see only the modification dates unless they go digging through the workflow history.

- Categories applied to a News Item appear on its page, but clicking them takes you to a search for all items (both blog-related and otherwise) having that category. This could be a bug or a feature, depending on your situation. However, the ordering of the search results is unpredictable, and that is definitely unhelpful.

The great thing about plain News Items is that there's a forward migration path. QuillsEnabled, which we'll explore later, can be layered atop an existing news-item-based blog with no migrations necessary and removed again if you decide to go back. Thus, a good strategy may be to start simple, with plain news items, and go after more features (and risk) as the need presents itself.

Scrawl: a blog with a view

One step up from plain News Items is Scrawl, a minimalist blog product that adds only two things:

- A custom Blog Entry type, which is actually just a copy of News Item
- A purpose-built Blog view that can be applied to folders or collections, which are otherwise used just as with raw News Items.
- Here are both additions in action:

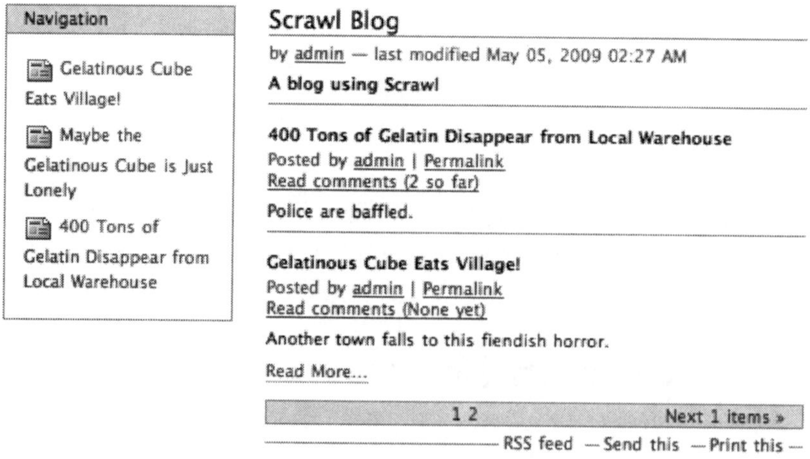

Scrawl's Blog Entry isn't quite a verbatim copy of News Item; Scrawl makes a few tweaks:

- Commenting is turned on for new Blog Entries, without which authors would have to enable it manually each time. The chances of that happening are slim, since it's buried on the **Edit** → **Settings** tab, and users seldom stray from the default tab when editing.
- Blog Entry's default view is a slightly modified version of News Item's: it shows the author's name and the posting date even to unauthenticated users—and in a friendly "Posted by Fred Finster" format. It also adds a **Permalink** link, lest you forfeit crosslinks from users who know no other way of finding an entry's address.

Calm your ringing phone by cloning types

Using a custom content type for blog entries—even if it's just a copy of an existing one—has considerable advantages. For one, you can match contributors' vocabulary: assuming contributors think of part of your site as a blog (which they probably will if the word "blog" appears anywhere onscreen), they won't find it obvious to add "news items" there. Adding a "blog entry," on the other hand, lines up naturally with their expectations. This little trick, combined with judicious use of the **Add new...** → **Restrictions...** feature to pare down their options, will save hours of your time in training and support calls.

A second advantage of a custom type is that it shows separately in Plone's advanced search. Visitors, like contributors, will identify better with the "blog entry" nomenclature. Plus, sometimes it's just plain handy to limit searches to only blogs.

This type-cloning technique isn't limited to blog entries; you can clone and rename any content type: just visit `portal_types` in the ZMI, copy and paste a type, rename it, and edit its **Title** and **Description** fields. One commonly cloned type is File. Many contributors, even experts in non-computer domains, aren't familiar with the word *file*. Cloning it to create PDF File, Word Document, and so on can go a long way toward making them comfortable using Plone.

Pros and cons of scrawl

Scrawl's biggest risk is lock-in: since it uses its own Blog Entry content type to store your entries, uninstalling it leaves them inaccessible. However, because the Blog Entry type is really just the News Item type, a migration script is easy to write:

```
# Turn all Blog Entries in a Plone site into News Items.
#
# Run by adding a "Script (Python)" in the ZMI (it doesn't matter
where) and pasting this in.

from Products.CMFCore.utils import getToolByName

portal_catalog = getToolByName(context, 'portal_catalog')
for brain in portal_catalog(portal_type='Blog Entry'):
    blog_entry = brain.getObject()  # Get the actual blog entry from
                                    # the catalog entry.
    blog_entry.portal_type = 'News Item'
    # Update the catalog so searches see the new info:
    blog_entry.reindexObject()
```

The reverse is also true: if you begin by using raw News Items and decide to switch to Scrawl, you'll need the reverse of the above script—just swap `'News Item'` and `'Blog Entry'`. If you have news items that shouldn't be converted to blog entries, your catalog query will have to be more specific, perhaps adding a `path` keyword argument, as in `portal_catalog(portal_type='News Item', path='/my-plone-site/blog-folder')`.

Aside from that, Scrawl is pretty risk-free. Its simplicity makes it unlikely to accumulate showstopping bugs or to break in future versions of Plone, and, if it does, you can always migrate back to news items or, if you have some programming skill, maintain it yourself—it's only 1,000 lines of code.

QuillsEnabled: blogging bells and whistles

Once upon a time, there was a blogging product called Quills. It was the most feature-rich blogging package in all the Plone kingdom, with trackbacks, pings, support for remote editors, and more. But alas, it introduced its own blog entry content type very different from News Item, so webmasters were forced to bear a substantial lock-in risk to get those features.

Today, we are fortunate enough to have QuillsEnabled, a rethinking of Quills without the risk of lock-in. Using marker-interface cleverness, QuillsEnabled provides all the features of Quills but using standard News Items. In fact, you can use any content type you like as blog entries—even more than one type in a single blog—and their fully rendered representations show in listings:

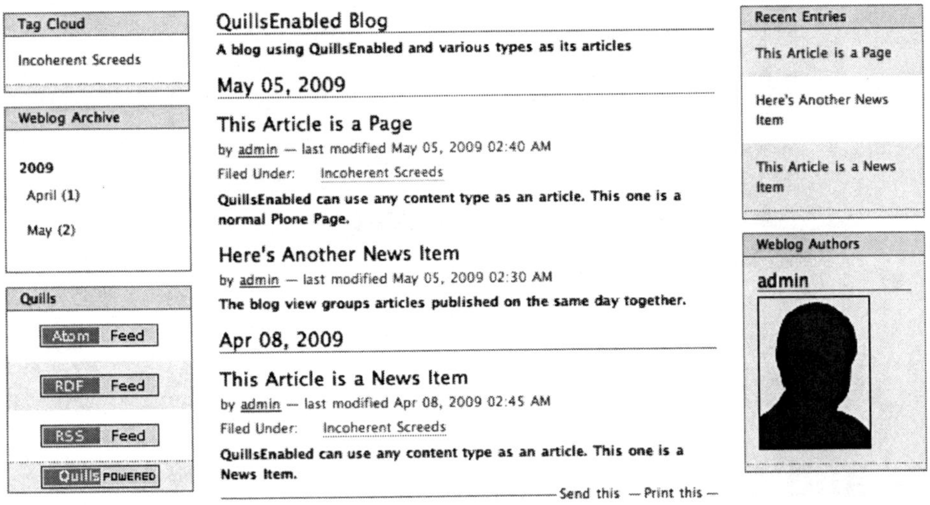

With lock-in thus addressed, QuillsEnabled is an easy recommendation for blogs that need bells and whistles like…

- A monthly archive of past entries (and within each month, a day-by-day archive)
- Atom and RDF syndication in addition to Plone's built-in RSS support
- An assortment of blog-like portlets, including a tag cloud, a list of recent comments, and a list of authors

QuillsEnabled is also very configurable on a per-blog basis:

Pros and cons of QuillsEnabled

QuillsEnabled is slightly easier to set up than Scrawl or a plain-news-item blog, since you don't have to build your own structure using collections and portlets. Instead, you just create a folder and choose **Activate blog** from its **Actions** menu. Everything is taken care of: pagination, an assortment of portlets, and month- and day-based organization of entries.

The downside of QuillsEnabled is a lack of any particular support for comments: they aren't indicated on listing pages except by the **Recent Comments** portlet, which shows only the subject line and gives no hint which entry they are attached to. Further, commenting isn't even turned on by default for new blog entries, making one more thing for contributors to remember. However, all of this has a straightforward solution: a pairing of QuillsEnabled with Scrawl, combining the best attributes of each.

QuillsEnabled + Scrawl: the perfect pair

Since QuillsEnabled lets you use any content type as a blog entry, why not use the Scrawl Blog Entry type? This gets you the easy setup of Quills along with its powerful listing, navigation, and publishing features, but you still get to enjoy the nicer entry templates and comment integration of Scrawl. Here's how to set it up:

1. Install both QuillsEnabled and Scrawl. The order of installation doesn't matter.
2. Make a new folder, and activate it as a QuillsEnabled blog.
3. Using the **Add new** menu, place restrictions on the folder so contributors can add only Scrawl blog entries.
4. In the **Weblog Admin** portlet, click **Configure Blog**. Set the **Default type** to "Blog Entry" so that clicking **Add Entry** in the admin portlet adds a Scrawl blog entry.

This gives you the best of both worlds:

- QuillsEnabled manages the listings, complete with monthly and daily breakdowns.
- Scrawl takes care of enabling comments on each new entry, so you don't need to trust or train your contributors to do it.
- Listings show how many comments each entry has.
- Individual entries use Scrawl's more informative custom view, which shows author name and posting date.
- Blog entries have their own type, which makes advanced searches easy to limit and comforts users with familiar vocabulary.

Forums with Ploneboard

While a blog is geared toward having one person post the lion's share of content and then a larger community make relatively short comments, a forum tends to be more egalitarian: someone—not necessarily the owner of the forum system—makes an initial post and then steps back to participate in the conversation as an equal. The difference, in practice, is slight: both forums and blogs have been evolving for more than a decade, and they have each absorbed many features of the other.

Among the implementations considered here, the most significant distinguisher is the richness of comments. In all the blog strategies we investigated, comments were limited to plain text and were either allowed or disallowed—nothing in between. In our forum, they can be rich—including styled text and attached files—and they can take advantage of Plone's powerful workflow engine, giving you the ability to vet comments before they appear to the public.

While there were some choices to make among blog implementations, the Ploneboard add-on is the clear winner in the forum space. From one of the world's foremost Plone development companies, it delivers a good balance of power and simplicity and receives prompt compatibility updates for new versions of Plone.

For better or worse, Ploneboard prescribes a four-level organization of forum content: **comments, conversations, forums**, and **message boards**.

Comments and conversations

A comment is an individual post, like a student might make to ask a question about an assignment. They can be edited, deleted, or temporarily hidden ("retracted") by administrators.

Conversations are threaded discussions made up of comments. They have two available views in the **Display** menu: **conversation_view**, which hides the nested structure of the exchange, and **threaded_conversation_view** (strangely not the default), which uses indentation to signify replies.

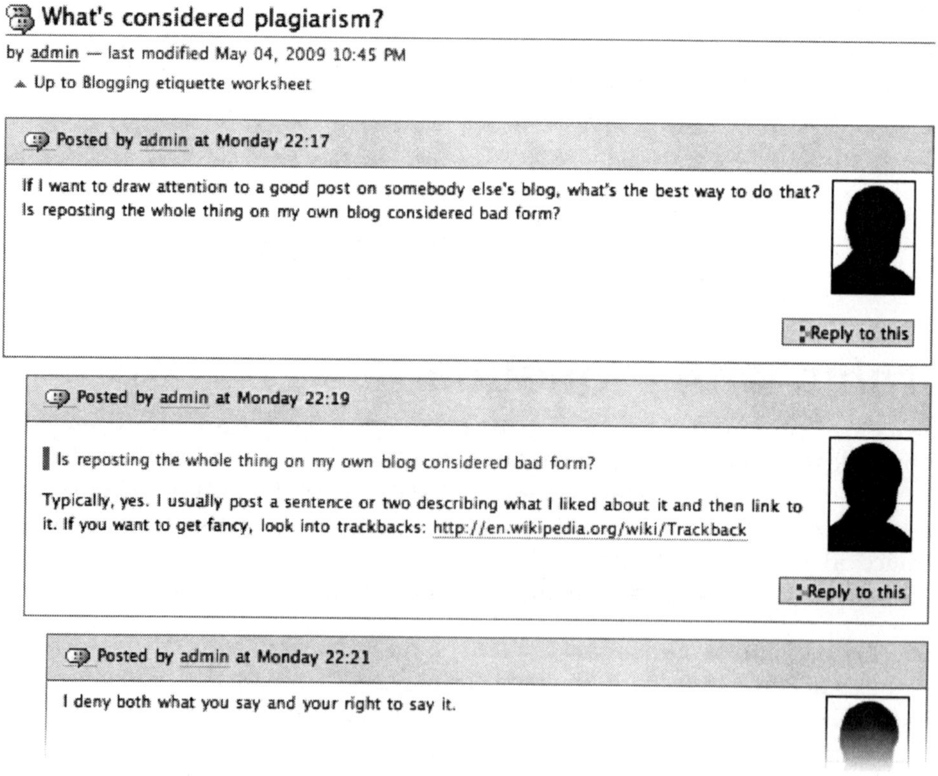

Forums

Forums group related conversations together. In an educational context, you might want to make a forum for each class assignment or lecture. Individual forums can also be assigned a category (distinct from Plone's standard categories), such as "Class Assignment".

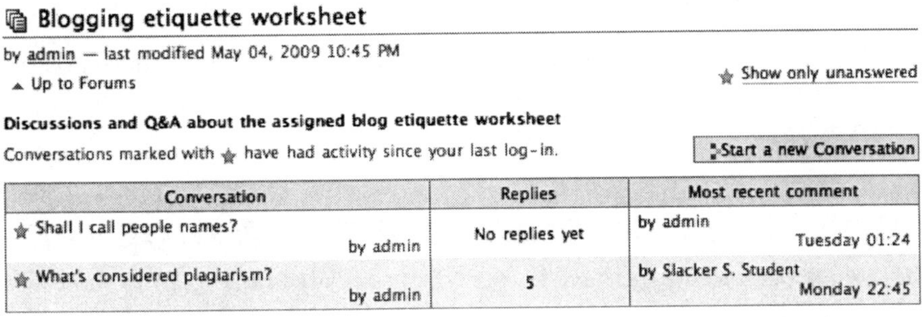

Message boards

Message boards are top-level containers of forums. A message board keeps track of what categories can be assigned to the forums within. A message board's front page groups its forums by categories, which appear as headings over each group. Uncategorized forums appear under a "General forums" heading.

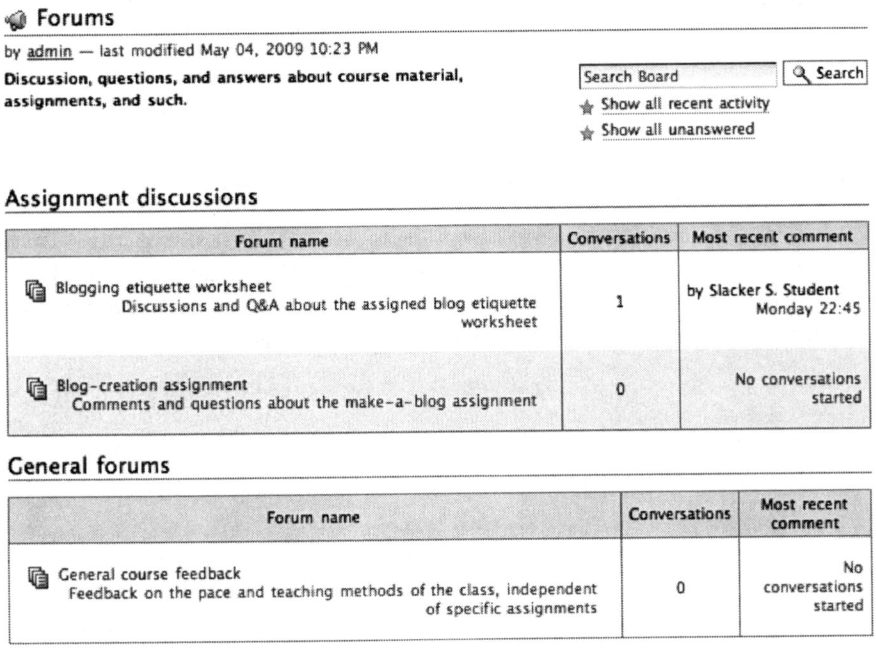

Harnessing Ploneboard's workflows

Ploneboard comes with an unusually thoughtful assortment of workflows:

- Conversations can be locked or open.
- Forums can be members-only, moderated, free-for-all, or private.
- Entire message boards can be shown or hidden.

These workflows are a handy way to control students' access without exposing less technically adept instructors to the potentially confusing **Sharing** tab. For some examples, read on.

Example 1: Moderated forums as drop boxes

How can we let students turn in work in a "drop box" fashion, so only the instructor can see it? The moderation workflow makes this easy:

1. Make a moderated forum called, for example, "Assignments".
2. Add a conversation named after a specific assignment: say, "Term Paper Drop Box".
3. Have students post their completed assignments as replies.

Students' posts aren't visible to each other, but site administrators (and instructors, if you play your **Sharing** tab cards right) can see them all. Comments allow file attachments, so this can stretch beyond even rich-text answers. And, while a comment is waiting for moderation (which it does forever in this scenario), its author can delete it and put up an improved version.

Example 2: Open forums for homework help

Open a forum to field questions about each assignment. This allows more efficient dissemination of answers to common questions without having to spend class time broadcasting them. In addition, it gives students the opportunity to help each other. Both potentials have proved true in university science classes.

Example 3: Forums for group work collaboration

Another practice that works well is to give each group in a group assignment a forum for internal communication.

Summary

In this chapter, we've examined and weighed three and a half ways of building a blog with Plone. We've also introduced the foremost forum implementation. Finally, we suggested ways to use these tools inside and outside the classroom as starting points for your own explorations. Happy communicating!

6

Embedding Audio and Video

In the past few years, schools of all sizes have embraced audio and video distribution of lecture materials, news, self-guided campus tours, and much more in the race for efficiency and attention. Conveniently, Plone has some great plug-in products that integrate these media smoothly into the experience of both end users and content contributors. In this chapter, you will...

- Learn how to publish audio and video all over to your Plone site, embedding it within portlets, including it within pages, and publishing podcasts that pack up your materials to go
- Find out how to triple your traffic using the iTunes Store
- See how to start your institution's presence on iTunes U, Apple's free distribution center for educational media

Meet the products

The most flexible and trouble-free solution for embedding audio and video in Plone is a product called `collective.flowplayer`. Written by long-time Plone developer Martin Aspeli, `collective.flowplayer` wraps a free Flash-based media player called, more concisely, "Flowplayer" in a thin coating of Plone goodness, allowing even contributors who don't speak HTML to add media to a site. The product makes it a point-and-click operation to add MP3 audio or Flash video (FLV) to any rich text field, as found in pages, events, or news items. It also allows for audio and video in portlets and automatically provides a player interface on MP3s or FLVs uploaded using the File content type.

Pros and cons of Flash video

Flash-encapsulated video has its ups and downs. One of the ups is extremely high browser penetration: some estimates place Flash on 98% of all browsers, making this format totally transparent for nearly all your audience. Both YouTube and Google Video use it, so, if your visitors can see those, they can see your movies as well. A second feature is that support for all of Flash's audio and video formats comes bundled with the plugin, so there are no "go find the right codec" (in other words, "give up on this web site") messages as sometimes occur with QuickTime.

One notable downside to FLV is that there is no Flash support yet on the iPhone, despite the device's popularity. Another downside is that few video workflows produce FLV natively, so a separate conversion step is needed. However, this is at most an annoyance, since free tools are readily available: for example, **ffmpeg** on Linux or **ffmpegX** on the Mac. Detailed instructions for encoding Flash with the latter are at `http://www.ffmpegx.com/flv.html`. Installing ffmpegX is a bit tricky—make sure that your account has administrative privileges and that there are no spaces in the path where you install it—but encoding is refreshingly simple.

Here is a taste of what `collective.flowplayer` can do: showing a movie in a portlet, another floated to the right within a page, and an audio player below the first paragraph:

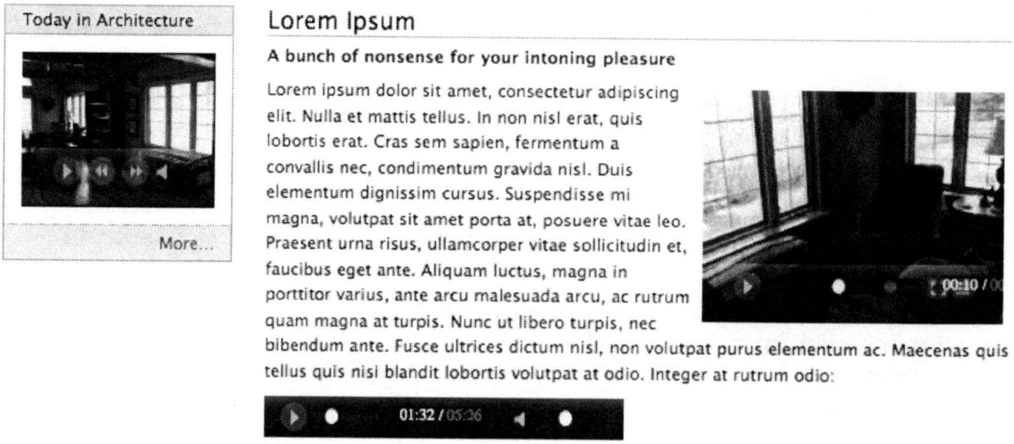

The other tool in our box is Plone4Artists Video, an older product, which we'll use solely to add podcasting support to folders and collections. It has some functional overlap with `collective.flowplayer`, which we will ignore, since `flowplayer`'s implementation provides smoother Plone integration.

We will also see how to include media the old-fashioned way, by manually entering `<embed>` and `<object>` tags, since this still has unique advantages in some situations.

Play standalone media

`collective.flowplayer`'s first trick is automatically adding an onscreen player to any MP3 or FLV content object. For example, add a File object anywhere in your Plone site, and upload an MP3 or FLV as its content. As soon as you click **Save**, you'll be greeted with a handy player of the sort shown either.

Conveniently, `flowplayer` also supports media stored outside your Plone site: instead of a File, create a Link object, and point it to the URL of an MP3 or FLV housed on another server. *Voilà*: the same player shows up.

Player options

Many aspects of the onscreen player can be tweaked on a per-Plone-site basis. The ZMI page at **your Plone site** → **portal_properties** → **flowplayer_properties** enumerates the options:

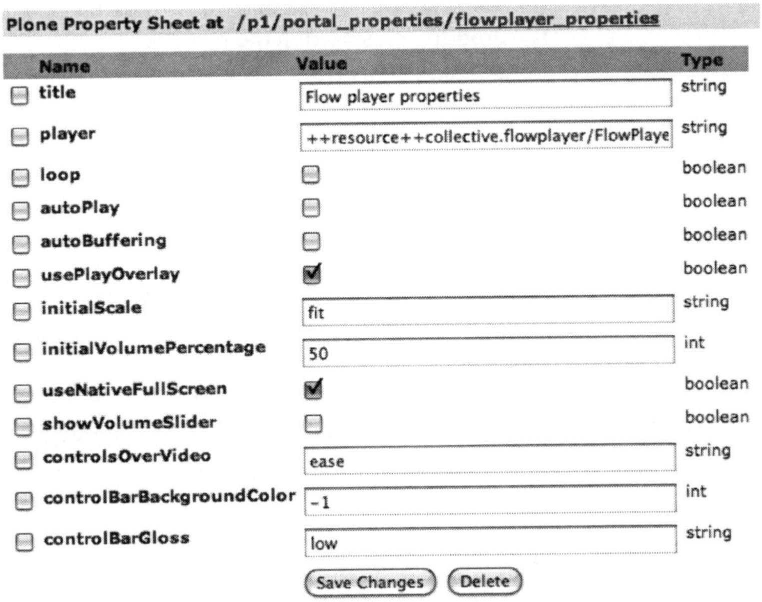

Option	Description
player	The URL of the Flash player to use. The main case for changing this is when you've purchased the commercial version of Flowplayer.
loop	If you are using a playlist (see below), loop back to the beginning after the last item finishes playing.
autoPlay	Make all players play immediately when the page is loaded.
autoBuffering	Begin downloading the media as soon as the page loads. (With **autoPlay** on, this makes no practical difference.)
usePlayOverlay	Show a **Play** button at the start of playlists.
initialScale	`fit`: Scale video to the size of the player (itself controlled by CSS or the size of the preview image—see below), but obey the proportions encoded in the FLV file. `half`: Scale to half the size of the player, obeying the encoded proportions. `orig`: Show video at the size encoded in the FLV file. If the player is constrained by CSS or the preview image, fall back to the `fit` setting. `scale`: Scale the video to the full size of the player, ignoring the proportions stored in the FLV file.
initialVolumePercentage	Initial volume level of players, from 0 to 100.
useNativeFullScreen	Use the fullscreen capability present in Flash 9.0.28.0 and later.
showVolumeSlider	Show a slider control to let the user change the volume.
controlsOverVideo	`ease`: Hide the controls whenever the mouse pointer remains still or is outside the video for 4 seconds. Move the pointer back over the video to show the controls again. `locked`: Always show the controls over top of the video. `no`: Show the controls below (not overlapping) the video.
controlBarBackgroundColor	The player's background color. This is an integer representation of a typical hexadecimal web color, like `#FF9933`. Hexadecimal conversion is left as an exercise to the reader.
controlBarGloss	Metallic shininess of the player controls: `low`, `high`, or `none`.

collective.flowplayer's default settings are reasonable, but turning on **showVolumeSlider** can't hurt; YouTube provides a volume control, and it sets expectations for many users. If you choose not to let users set the volume, consider at least changing **initialVolumePercentage** to 100 so users of MacBooks, which have notoriously quiet audio hardware, will have a fighting chance.

Embed media in pages

collective.flowplayer's greatest strength is embedding audio and video within the text of pages, news items, and other pieces of content. Its editing interface integrates with Kupu, Plone's default WYSIWYG editor, in a way that's minimally invasive and thus unlikely to break your site in the future. Specifically, it uses CSS classes combined with JavaScript magic that executes on page load.

Embed audio

Embedding audio within a page (or any other rich-text-carrying piece of content) goes like so:

1. Within the **Body Text** field, add a link to an MP3, using any of Kupu's various link-making buttons. Or, in HTML mode, add markup like this:

   ```
   <a href="some/folder/gerbils-shouting.mp3">Gerbils Shouting
      (Any contents of this tag will be replaced.)</a>
   ```

2. It doesn't matter whether the link points to an address inside or outside your Plone site or even to another server altogether; the Flowplayer is equally happy to pull data from anywhere.

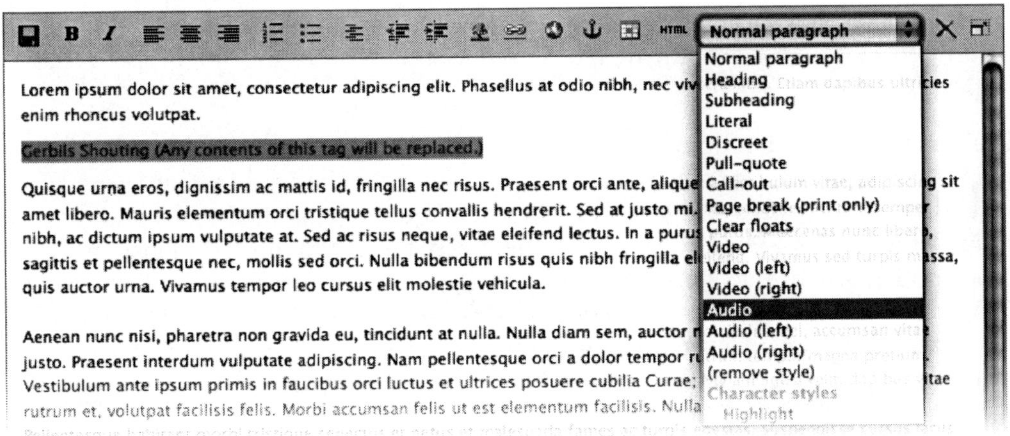

3. Apply one of the Audio styles to the link. In WYSIWYG-editing mode, select the link, and choose one of the styles from the pop-up menu. The Audio (right) and Audio (left) styles float the player to the right or left, respectively, while plain Audio renders it as a block element, kicking the following content down to the next line. Behind the scenes, applying the styles adds CSS classes like this:

   ```
   <a class="autoFlowPlayer audio image-right" href="some/folder/
   gerbils-shouting.mp3">Gerbils Shouting</a>
   ```

4. HTML-savvy content jockeys can feel free to add the above manually. They may also add a minimal CSS class to shrink the player to just a disembodied Play icon.

Of course, simply applying some CSS to an anchor tag does not an interactive audio player make. That's where the clever part comes in. `collective.flowplayer` registers some JavaScript for inclusion on every page which, when the page loads, searches for occurrences of the magical CSS classes and inserts Flash players at appropriate spots. (The inquisitive can see the JavaScript registrations in the ZMI, toward the bottom of `portal_javascripts`.) The advantage of this approach is a good prospect of future compatibility. Since there are no player-specific additions to the page markup, other players could straightforwardly be substituted if Flowplayer or `collective.flowplayer` were ever to become unsupported. In the absolute worst case, the embedded media would fail to appear, but the rest of the page would keep working fine.

Embed video

Embedding FLV-wrapped video is done much the same as audio, except that an image takes the place of the arbitrary text inside the link. As with an embedded YouTube video, the image is used as a preview of the video, and a click begins playback.

The preview image determines the size of the player, which isn't smart enough to snap to the right size on its own. Because Plone limits embedded images to one of several predefined sizes—200, 400, or 768 pixels square being the largest and most suitable for movies—your video is also effectively limited to those dimensions. If you need another size or two, look into the `plone.app.imaging` package, which lets you define new ones using a site-wide control panel. If, however, you need more than a few new sizes, consider the method described in the *Embed media manually* section, just ahead, so you don't over-clutter Kupu's **Size** menu and confuse your content contributors.

1. In a page's **Body Text** field, add an image to use as a preview of your video. It should be the size you want the video to appear and inserted **inline**, rather than floated right or left.
2. Select the image, and make it a link to your FLV file.
3. Apply one of the **Video** styles to the linked image. As with the **Audio** styles, **Video (right)** or **(left)** float the movie and cause text to wrap around it, while plain **Video** places the movie on its own line. The complete markup for a right-floated video looks like this, for the HTML-inclined:

```
<div class="autoFlowPlayer video image-right">
    <a href="some/folder/gerbils-dancing.flv">
        <img class="image-inline" src="some/folder/gerbils-
dancing.png/image_preview" alt="Gerbils Dancing" />
    </a>
</div>
```

4. You could also omit the `div` and apply all the classes to the anchor tag, but the above is what Kupu generates.

Embed media manually

Though you can't beat its convenience for content providers, there are several situations in which `collective.flowplayer` won't work. For instance…

- YouTube videos, which are delivered in the form of SWF files, bring their own player with them and thus cannot be played through Flowplayer.
- Adobe Presenter, a popular tool which converts PowerPoint presentations for the web, also outputs standalone SWF files.
- QuickTime movies must be played by the QuickTime browser plugin rather than Flowplayer.

Fortunately, we can still embed all of these media in Plone rich text fields; we just need to use the `<object>` and `<embed>` tags by hand.

Enable the tags

For reasons of security and standards-compliance, Plone does not allow `<object>` and `<embed>` in content by default. Before we can use them, we must lift those restrictions:

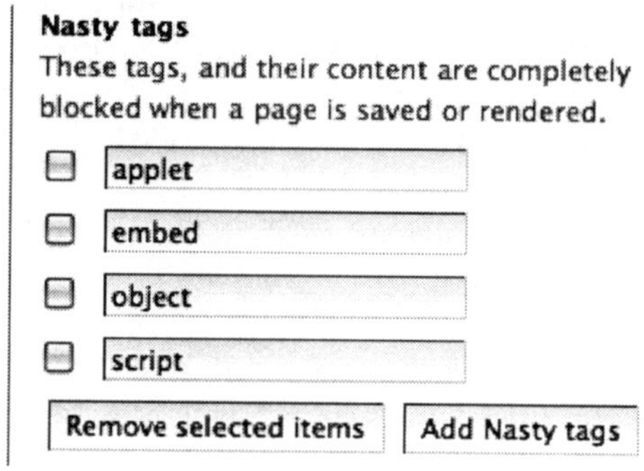

1. In **Site Setup** → **HTML Filtering**, remove `object` and `embed` from the **Nasty tags** section.
2. Also remove `object` and `param` from the **Stripped tags** section.
3. Since the `embed` tag isn't strictly part of the XHTML specification, add it to the **Custom tags** section. (To make a blank field appear, click **Add Custom tags**.)
4. Click **Save**.

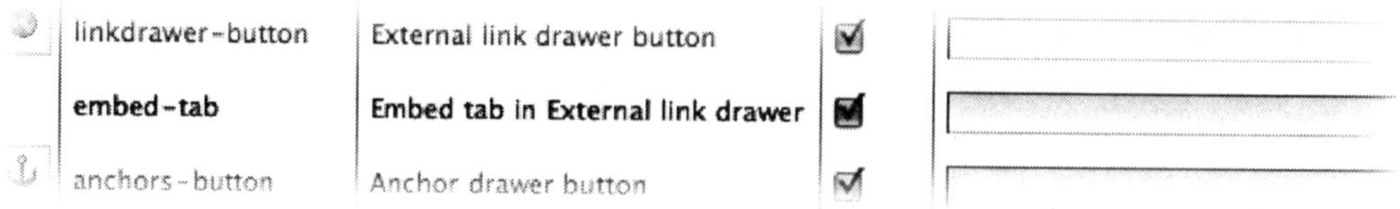

Finally, enable a new piece of Kupu glitz to make your content contributors' jobs easier:

5. In **Site Setup** → **Visual editor**, visit the **Toolbar** tab, and turn on the **embed-tab** button. Click **Save**.

> **Beware cross-site scripting attacks**
>
> If you enable these tags, be sure that you trust your content editors. Though they are unlikely to cause problems by accident, malicious use of this new power could introduce potentially dangerous scripts into your site. For example, a student making a rich-text forum post (as in the *Blogs and Forums* chapter) could embed a specially crafted SWF file, which could in turn use ActionScript to execute arbitrary JavaScript in the context of the current page for other people, passing sensitive data to an outsider. Flash does provide some protection against this: a parameter, `allowscriptaccess`, which can disable scripting. However, there is no way in the context of Plone and Kupu to force content editors to set it to a safe setting. Thus, if you want to enable manual embedding of objects, you should not allow untrusted users to edit rich text fields.

Insert the media

Once the initial setup is done, actually embedding media is simple:

1. While editing using Kupu, click the external link button (which looks like the Earth).

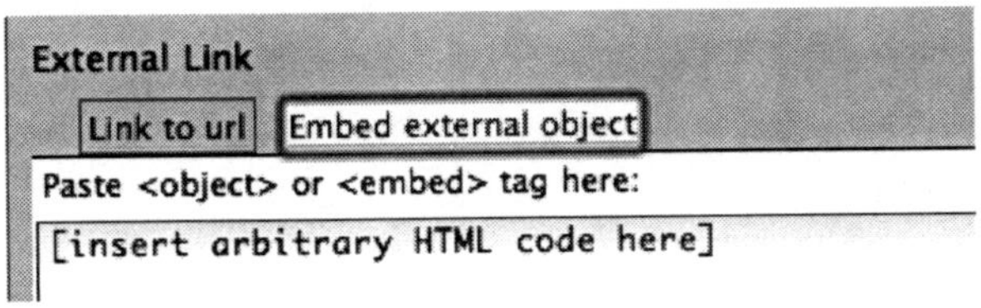

2. Click the newly enabled **Embed external object** tab.
3. In the large text field below, paste the code to embed whatever media you wish. Most online video services offer the proper embedding code in a conspicuous place. For instance, YouTube recommends something like this:

```
<object width="425" height="344">
    <param name="movie" value="http://www.youtube.com/v/
zSgiXGELjbc&hl=en_US&fs=1&"></param>
    <param name="allowFullScreen" value="true"></param>
    <param name="allowscriptaccess" value="never"></param>
    <embed src="http://www.youtube.com/v/zSgiXGELjbc&hl=en_
US&fs=1&"
        type="application/x-shockwave-flash"
allowscriptaccess="always"
        allowfullscreen="true" width="425" height="344"></embed>
</object>
```

Any other SWF file would be represented similarly. Note that in the preceding, we set `allowscriptaccess` to `never`, its safest setting.

4. To embed a QuickTime movie, use slightly different code:

```
<object CLASSID="clsid:02BF25D5-8C17-4B23-BC80-D3488ABDDC6B"
        width="320" height="256" CODEBASE="http://www.apple.com/
qtactivex/qtplugin.cab">
    <param name="src" value="http://quicktime.tc.columbia.edu/
users/lrf10/movies/sixties.mov">
    <param name="qtsrc" value="http://quicktime.tc.columbia.edu/
users/lrf10/movies/sixties.mov">
    <param name="autoplay" value="true">
    <param name="loop" value="false">
    <param name="controller" value="true">
    <embed src="http://quicktime.tc.columbia.edu/users/lrf10/
movies/sixties.mov"
         qtsrc="http://quicktime.tc.columbia.edu/users/lrf10/
movies/sixties.mov"
         width="320" height="256" autoplay="true" loop="false"
controller="true"
         pluginspage="http://www.apple.com/quicktime/"></embed>
</object>
```

5. Once the embedding code is finished, click **OK**.
6. Make any further edits to the rich text, and click **Save**. Your media should appear immediately.

Media in portlets

In addition to embedding it in rich text fields, `collective.flowplayer` also provides for showing video and audio in portlets:

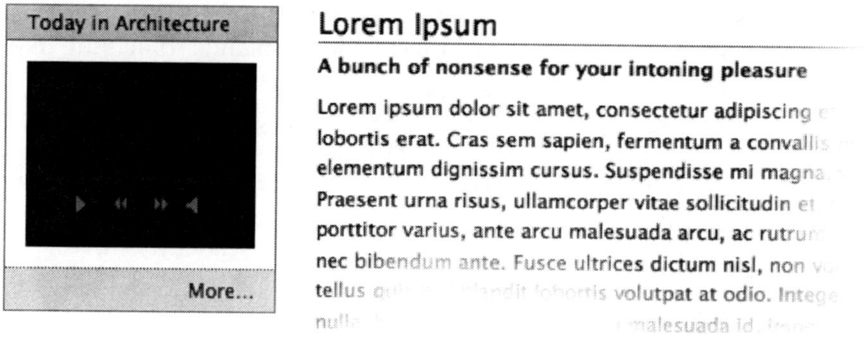

Click **Manage Portlets** on the page or folder where you want the portlet to appear, and add a **Video player** portlet. Despite its name, the portlet will play both audio and video. It allows you to set its title and splash image and gives you the option of a **More...** link pointing to the source material. Selecting a folder or collection rather than a single piece of media creates a portlet that loops through the media in the container. It also adds buttons to the control bar for navigating back and forth, as shown earlier.

Podcasting

Podcasting is a widely-adopted mechanism for subscribing to periodically released content. Most often used to pull audio and video onto mobile devices, podcasts are a burgeoning medium in the higher education space, benefitting faculty and students alike. Large, well-designed studies on educational podcasting are still lacking, but experience suggests the following:

- Students use podcasts of lectures mostly to review class material, not as a substitute for coming to class. Roger Santos of UC Davis's Academic Technology Services reported no sign of decreased attendance in 2006-2007, even though use of their lecture podcasting service rose 154% over the previous year (`http://technews.ucdavis.edu/news2.cfm?id=1562`). And Caton Roberts of UW-Madison reported a negligible effect on attendance (`https://tle.wisc.edu/solutions/lecturing/will-podcasting-my-lectures-reduce-class-attendance`).
- Podcasts are particularly helpful to students who speak English as a non-native language; they can pause and repeat sections as many times as needed.
- Released to the public, a high-quality course podcast can be an excellent advertisement for your school. For many high school students, a survey of lecture podcasts helps form their first cut of colleges to consider.

The best solution for podcasting from Plone is Plone4Artists Audio. Based on the same "sub-typing" framework as Plone4Artists Calendar (used in the *Calendaring* chapter) Plone4Artists Audio is based on the idea of tagging folders and collections as **Audio Containers**. Once so tagged, a container gains an RSS icon, which exposes a feed of all the MP3s and Ogg Vorbis files within—a simple and functional podcast. Note the RSS feed icon in the upper right:

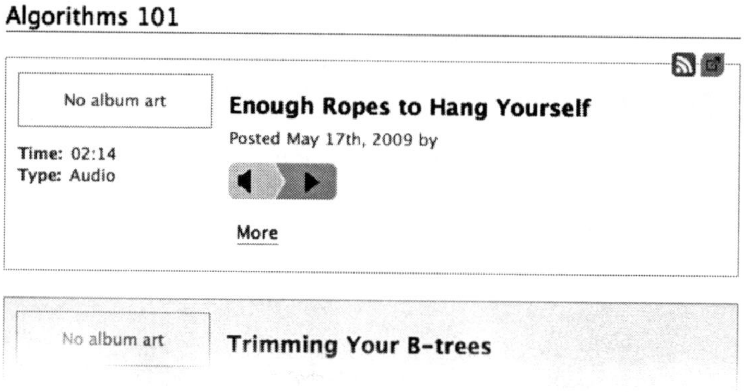

Installing Plone4Artists Audio is a familiar matter of adding `p4a.ploneaudio` to both the `eggs` and `zcml` sections of your `buildout.cfg`. Also be sure to add `Products.fatsyndication`, which provides the RSS infrastructure that P4A Audio uses.

```
[instance]
eggs =
    ...other eggs...
    p4a.ploneaudio
    Products.fatsyndication
zcml =
    ...other zcml entries...
    p4a.ploneaudio
    Products.fatsyndication
```

Then, to set up a folder or collection as a podcast...

1. Add MP3s or Ogg Vorbis (`.ogg`) files to the container. If you added these files to your Plone site before Plone4Artists Audio was installed, make sure each has the **Audio** sub-type applied—you may have to visit the **Sub-type** menu on each and apply it manually. Otherwise, the file will be omitted from the podcast.

2. Make sure the container has an appropriate workflow state (typically Published), and advertise the URL pointed to by the RSS icon as your podcast's URL.

Listeners can then subscribe to your podcast by entering the URL in iTunes or any other podcatching software:

Advertising on the iTunes store

Though podcasting is a combination of open standards and thus vendor-neutral, Apple's iTunes Store has become the de facto clearinghouse for all things podcast-related: it is not unusual for a general-interest podcast to receive upwards of 70% of its referrals from the Store. Thus, if you would like to expand your audience beyond a roomful of students, this is the place to be. Fortunately, adding your content to the iTunes Store is free and easy:

1. Install iTunes if you don't have it already.
2. Go to `https://phobos.apple.com/WebObjects/MZFinance.woa/wa/publishPodcast`. You'll be sent through a redirection or two and, if all goes well, land in iTunes at a prompt to enter your podcast URL. Do so, and then follow the provided instructions.

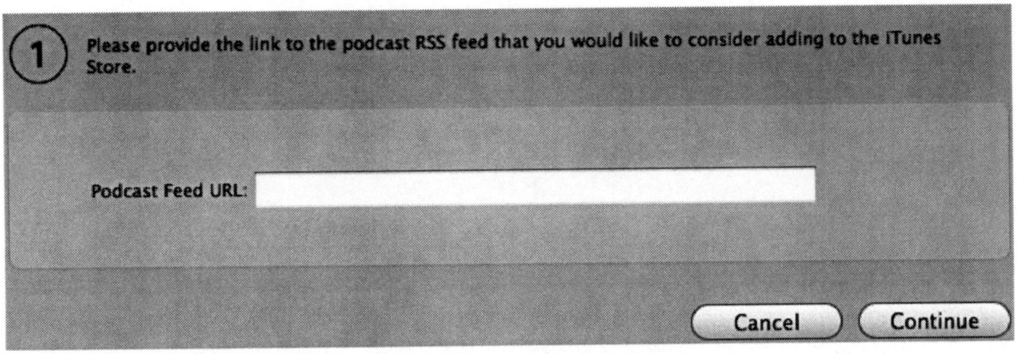

3. Wait a few days for Apple to review your submission. After that, your podcast should be available under the Podcasts section in the iTunes Store!

iTunes U

In response to the growing popularity of podcasts in higher education, Apple has dedicated a special section of the iTunes Store just for educational and other cultural institutions, such as museums and public television stations. iTunes U presences are established at the organizational level and are typically much more polished than solo-flying lecture podcasts, but if podcasts begin to catch on at your school, iTunes U is a great way to achieve even more visibility.

See `http://education.apple.com/itunesu/` to get started on an iTunes U presence for your institution.

Summary

In this chapter, we've seen how to integrate audio and video with Plone: weaving it into pages, populating portlets, and podcasting it to the world. We've covered the mechanics of the processes and learned many real-world tips to better your users' experience and increase the visibility of your published content.

7

Creating Forms Fast

It's a common problem for web developers: someone needs a one-off form for an event registration, a survey, or a field trip sign-off. But putting together a robust implementation—with proper validation, useful error messages, and good-looking layout—can be quite a time sink. Even assuming a good form framework, it remains a programming task, drawing your development hours away from infrastructural work that supports the long-term success of your site. Wouldn't it be nice if your content contributors could build forms as needed, without waiting for or drawing on development resources? PloneFormGen gives your contributors this very independence by providing a general-purpose, through-the-web tool for building forms.

PloneFormGen is one of the best-maintained products in the Plone universe and a true community effort. Managed by Steve McMahon, a well-respected Plone developer, the project draws liberally from a long line of other successful products: its mail-sending comes from PloneFormMailer, its icons from Formulator, its installation and testing machinery from RichDocument, and its form viewing and editing from Archetypes itself. PloneFormGen is always up to date with the latest Plone version, and bugs are squashed quickly and thoroughly. In an earlier chapter, we compared products to puppies. This one is a show-quality specimen.

Install PloneFormGen

Install PloneFormGen by adding `Products.PloneFormGen` to your buildout, as per usual. Run buildout, then start Zope back up, and install the product using the **Add-on Products** control panel. In addition, if you think you might use **Rich Text** or **Date/Time** Fields on forms targeted at unauthenticated users, throw the following switches to load the supporting JavaScript for everyone, not just people who are logged in:

1. In the **Zope Management Interface** (**ZMI**), navigate to the `portal_css` tool inside your Plone site.
2. Under the `member.css` stylesheet, the **Condition** field should read `not: portal/portal_membership/isAnonymousUser`. Clear this field. This will make the CSS in `member.css` load for everyone, making your pages a bit larger to download but more functional.
3. Go to the `portal_javascript` tool, which lives beside the `portal_css` tool.
4. Enable the pop-up calendar for the **Date/Time** field by finding the `calendar_formfield.js` section and clearing out its **Condition** field.
5. Enable the Kupu visual editor for the **Rich Text** field by finding all the Kupu-related scripts—they'll all have something like `python:portal.kupu_library_tool.isKupuEnabled...` in their **Condition fields**—and adding an `allowAnonymous=True` argument to the `isKupuEnabled` call. So `python:portal.kupu_library_tool.isKupuEnabled(REQUEST=request)` should become `python:portal.kupu_library_tool.isKupuEnabled(allowAnonymous=True, REQUEST=request)`.

A tour of PloneFormGen

PloneFormGen represents a form as a folder and fields as items within it, which lets it inherit a lot of its user interface "for free" from Plone. To start a new form, pull down the **Add new** menu anywhere in a Plone site, and choose **Form Folder**.

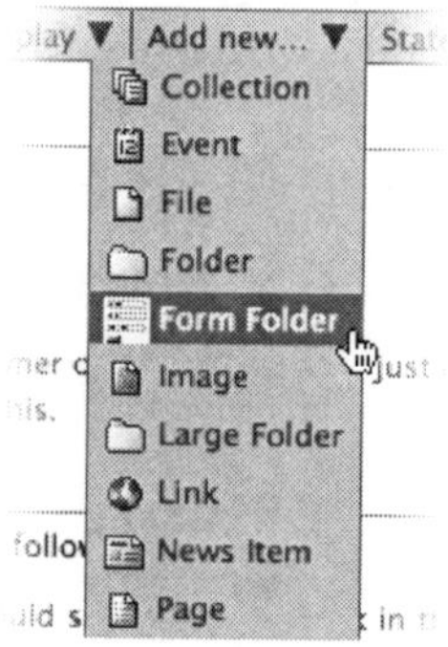

> **Easing the mental mapping for users**
>
> Though it simplifies the codebase, the way forms behave like folders is not always intuitive for less technical users; some will need a bit of training and acclimation. For larger organizations, it can help to have a Form Czar or two: community-minded power users with people skills who can render informal first-tier support and training.

After you add a form folder, a page of options will appear. For now, just set the **Title** to **Contact Us**, and click **Save** at the bottom of the page. To give you a jumping-off point, PloneFormGen adds not just an empty form folder but enough within it to provide a simple contact form: email address, subject, and a field for comments. If this is what you want, great—stop here! If not, click the subtle little wrench icon to the far right of the **Contact Us** title, and we'll see how PloneFormGen works behind the scenes:

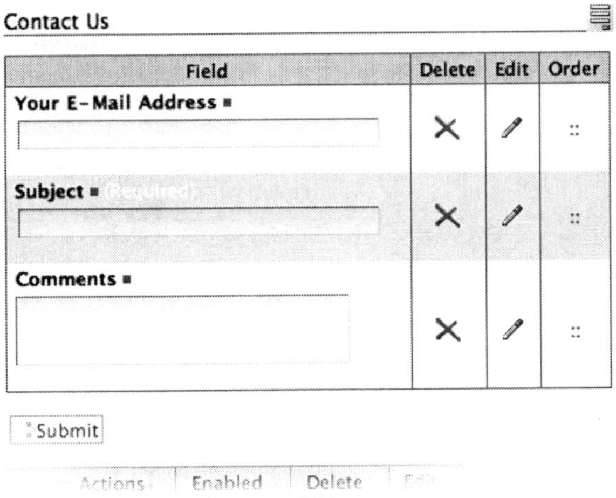

Clicking the wrench brings us into **quick-edit mode**, which bears a resemblance to the completed form but also lets you change it. Initially, you'll see the three fields PloneFormGen automatically added to your form folder and below, two mysterious tables titled "Form Actions" and "Thanks Pages" which we'll explore in a moment. You can delete the fields, edit them, or, by dragging beneath the **Order** column, change their order in the form.

This is a fine time to try adding some of the other fifteen types of fields PloneFormGen includes. Pull down the **Add new** menu and explore! As you play, you can always click the icon in the upper right corner (variously a wrench or a tiny representation of a form) to switch between quick-edit mode and the form as seen by visitors. As a reference, the next section summarizes the available field types.

Field types

PloneFormGen ships with a wide variety of fields. Here's the full menagerie:

Field Type	Description
Checkbox	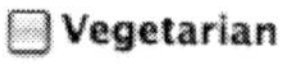 Can be either checked or not, and allows customization of what is returned in each state. Offers a validator that can constrain submissions to checked or not checked, which can be useful for "I accept these terms" click-through agreements.
Date/Time Field	 Collects a date and a time. If the time is left blank, defaults to midnight. Though the range of years it offers can be customized, this isn't well enforced, so be sure to use a **Custom Validator** expression on its **Overrides** tab if you need to enforce a certain range.
Decimal Number Field	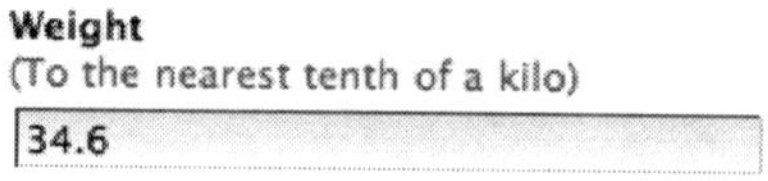 Can constrain its values between an entered minimum and maximum without you needing to write a custom validation expression.
Fieldset Folder	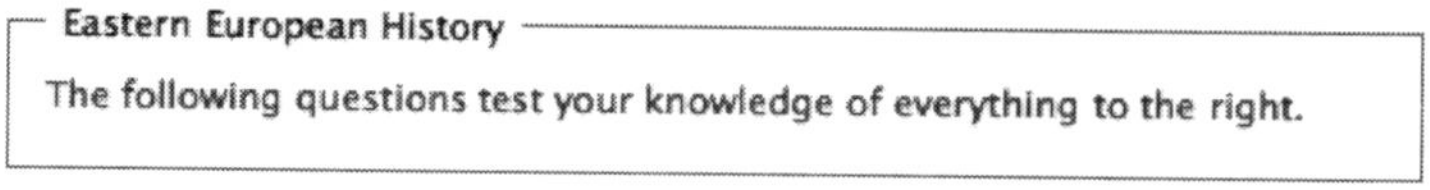 Not really a field at all, this is actually a group in which more fields can reside. In the final rendering of the form, the fieldset folder will be turned into an HTML `<fieldset>` tag surrounding its contents.
File Field	 Allows uploading a file and capping uploads at a certain size. Handy for turn-in forms, though keep in mind that **save data adapters** (see later) don't capture files. Use with a **mail adapter** instead.

Field Type	Description
Label Field	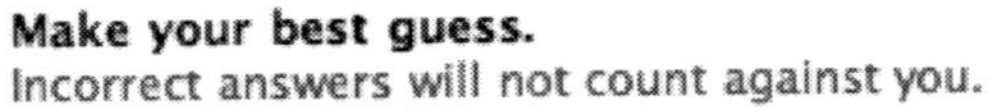 Just a label and, like all fields, some optional help text. Useful for displaying lengthy instructions at the top of a fieldset folder.
Lines Field	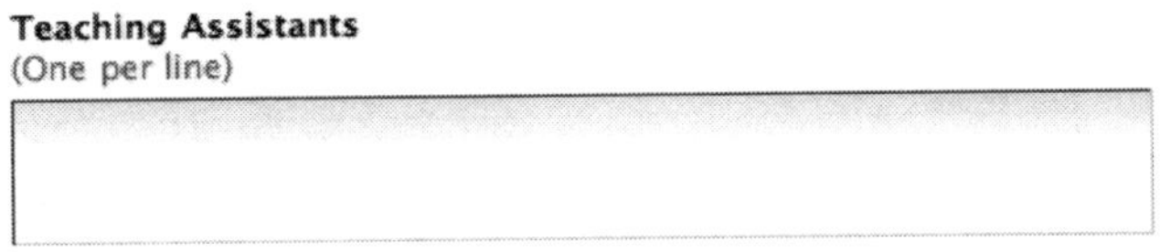 Collects multiple lines of plain text, which are separated by newline characters in saved input.
Multi-Select Field	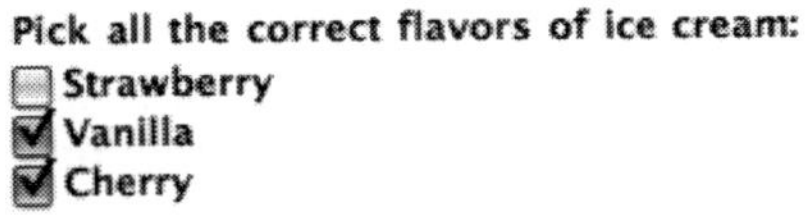 Presents a choice of zero or more options from a list. Also has an alternative format as a text field that requires users to hold down a modifier key to select multiple options. Users tend to have difficulty with this format.
Password Field	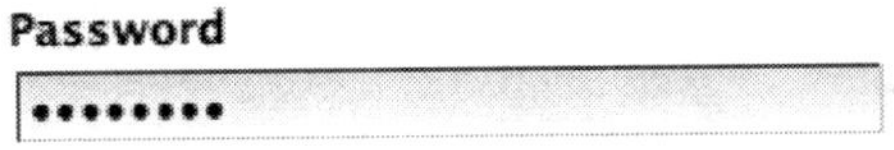 Like the string field, except that the input is not displayed.
Rating-Scale Field	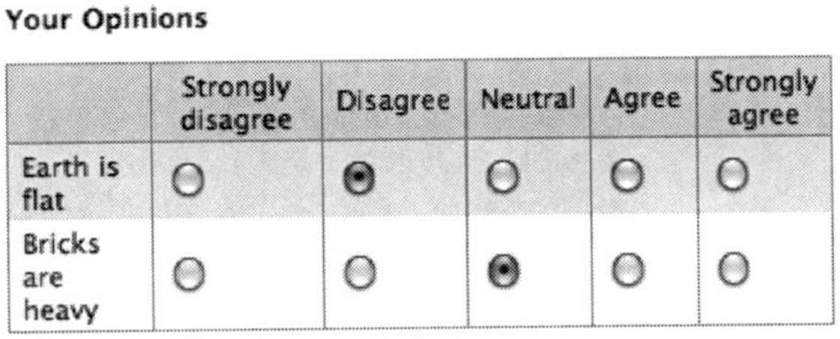 Great for Likert scales or, since the column labels can be customized, any other grid-based set of inputs that all share the same small number of responses
Rich Label Field	 A piece of arbitrary HTML. Handy for instructions in the middle of a form or at the beginning of a fieldset.

Field Type	Description
Rich Text Field	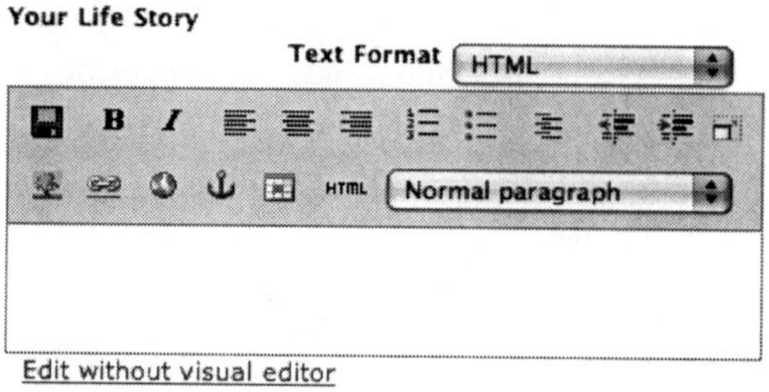 Collects HTML from the user through a visual editor.
Selection Field	 Presents a choice of a single item from a list. Has an alternative incarnation as a pop-up menu, which makes sense when the list is large.
String Field	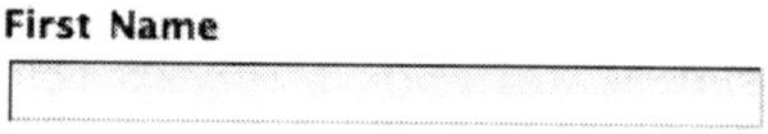 Collects a single line of text, optionally with a length restriction. Also has a wide variety of validators built in, matching against the formats of email addresses, phone numbers, URLs, ZIP codes, and more.
Text Field	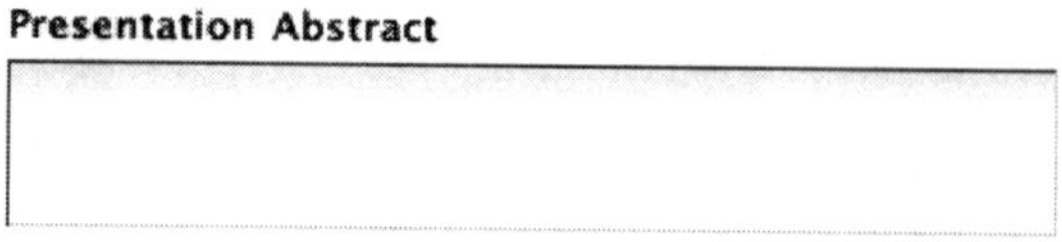 Collects plain text. Differs from the lines field mostly in philosophy: the lines field considers each line to be an independent piece of information, while this considers even multi-line input one big blob. This is evinced by the availability of a whole-field length restriction on this field, absent from the other.
Whole Number Field	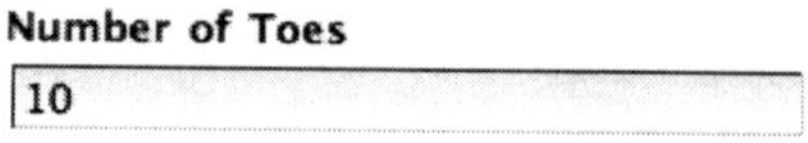 Accepts numbers without decimals. Can require its input to be in a range you specify.

Form Actions

When in quick-edit mode, you'll see a **Form Actions** table below the list of fields. This is where you can choose what to do with the form data once it's submitted. PloneFormGen ships with a variety of possible actions, provided by modules called **action adapters**, and third-party products can add more. The next few sections describe the out-of-the-box choices.

Emailing submissions

The **mailer adapter** emails the contents of the form to one or more people. A new form gets one of these by default, but be sure to fill out at least the **Recipient's e-mail address** (by clicking the **Edit** pencil in quick-edit mode), or an error will occur on form submission.

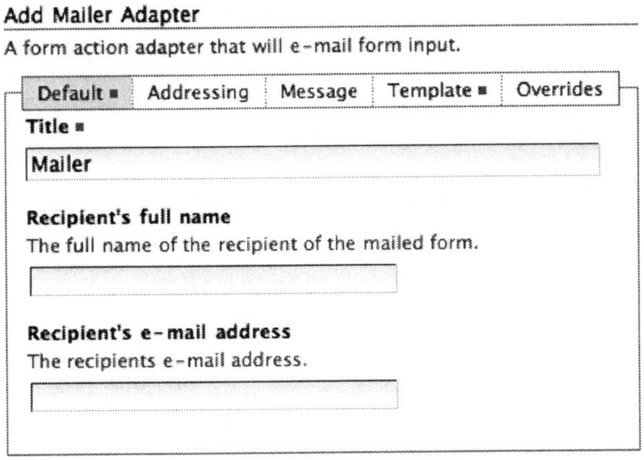

Note that you can set the default recipient for new forms in **Site Setup** → **PloneFormGen** → **Mail Addressing**. You'll need a mail server properly configured under **Site Setup** → **Mail**.

> **Encryption with GPG**
>
> Since email is an insecure transport and Plone doesn't support mail delivery over SSL, PloneFormGen provides for encryption via GNU Privacy Guard (GPG), in case you do need to mail sensitive data. To activate GPG support, install the command-line version of GPG, restart Zope, and an **Encryption** tab will appear on all mail adapters. From this tab, set which public key should be used to encrypt the sent messages. For more details about using GPG with PloneFormGen, see `README_GPG.txt` in the PloneFormGen package.

Saving submissions in the ZODB

The **save data adapter** stores form submissions in the ZODB for later export as a comma- or tab-delimited file, which in turn can be loaded into a spreadsheet or database for further manipulation. To add a save data adapter, pull down the **Add new** menu just as when adding a field, and choose **Save Data Adapter**. It will automatically catch all future submissions.

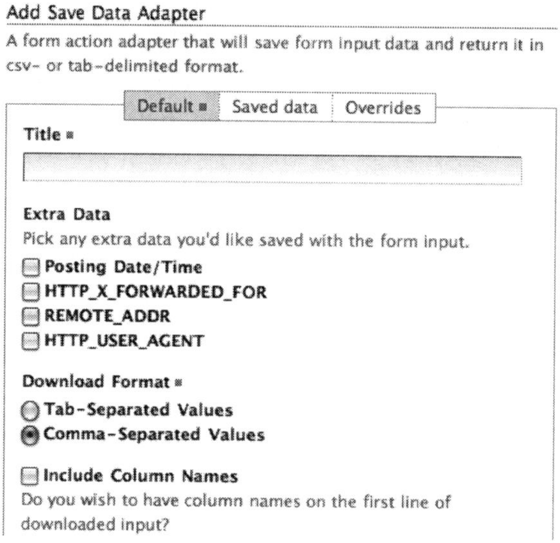

To download the saved submissions, navigate to the adapter (for example, via the form's **Contents** tab), click the adapter's **View** tab if it isn't already selected, and use the **Click here to get the saved input** link. Be sure to warn your users not to click the **Clear Saved Input** button instead, as it throws everything away without even a prompt for confirmation.

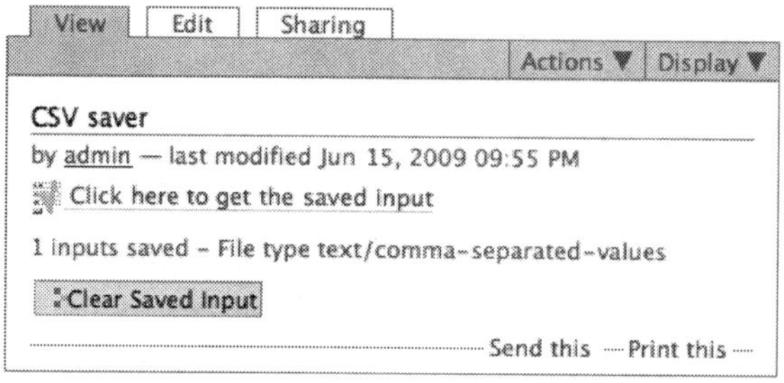

What if I hit the Clear Saved Input button accidentally?

If you do hit it, there's still hope. Head into the ZMI, navigate to the root level of your Plone site, and click the **Undo** tab. From there, you should see a transaction something like `/my-plone-site/fg_savedata_view_p3 by LucyTheUnlucky`. Check its box, hit **Undo**, and, with any luck, you data should be restored. Undo doesn't always work, so it's a good idea to always keep a mailer adapter in your forms as a backup—you can have as many action adapters as you wish.

Viewing and editing stored data is also supported, via the **Saved data** tab. The display is a bit crude so far, just one line per submission with commas between fields:

```
Alex@example.com,Great site!,This is the best site I've ever seen.
Bob@example.com,Poor site!,This is the worst site I've ever visited.
```

However, it can be useful for deleting test inputs and spam. At a pinch, you can even leave data there long-term, where anyone with the proper permissions can view it.

A warning about editing live forms

If you remove or reorder fields after a form has begun collecting data, PloneFormGen isn't smart enough to rearrange the data in parallel: when you download it, the field names won't match up with the data collected before the changes. To work around this, download a copy of the data and click **Clear Saved Input** before deleting or reordering fields.

Doing custom processing

If the previous two adapters don't fit the bill, here's your opportunity to build your own. A **custom script adapter** is basically a Python script that executes after the form is submitted and cleanly validated.

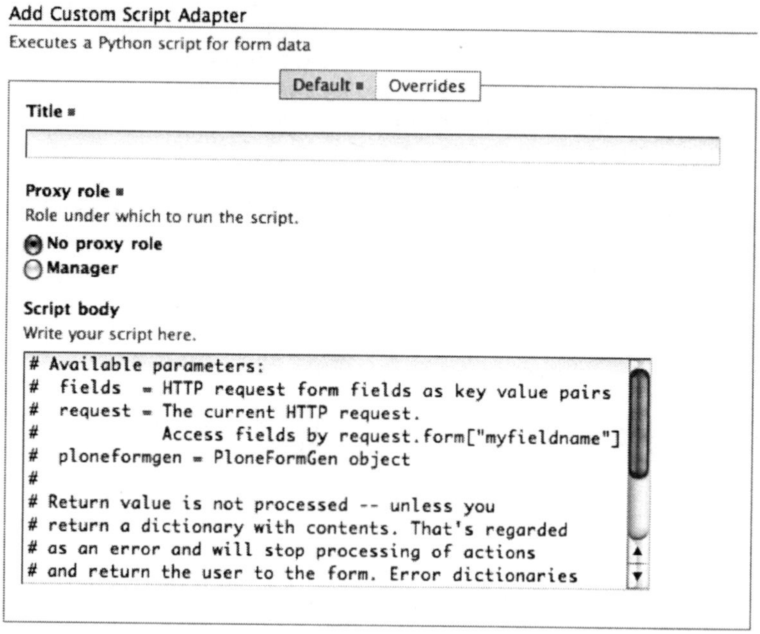

Anything is possible here, within the bounds of Restricted Python. Common uses include saving to a relational database or sending the data to another system via XML-RPC. There is also the option to set a **proxy role** on the script—in other words, to give the script Manager permissions (for example) while it runs. This can be useful for socking away bits of data in Zope objects where the user filling out the form shouldn't otherwise be allowed to venture.

> **What is Restricted Python?**
>
> Restricted Python is a subset of the Python language that limits the harm a script writer can do. This is the language exposed by `python` TALES expressions and Script (Python) objects in the ZMI, designed to allow the delegation of some scripting abilities to contributors who may not be entirely trusted.
>
> In Restricted Python, the importing of modules and items from them is limited, and many language features—like classes, nested functions, and even variable names beginning with an underscore—are disallowed. Because each attribute or item access (basically, each occurrence of a period or square bracket) triggers a security check, Restricted Python runs significantly slower than unrestricted, but it still saves your users broad swaths of time.

Some helpful documentation shows up in the **Script body** field when you make a new custom script adapter:

```
# Available parameters:
#  fields  = HTTP request form fields as key value pairs
#  request = The current HTTP request.
#            Access fields by request.form["myfieldname"]
#  ploneformgen = PloneFormGen object
#
# Return value is not processed -- unless you
# return a dictionary with contents. That's regarded
# as an error and will stop processing of actions
# and return the user to the form. Error dictionaries
# should be of the form {'field_id':'Error message'}

assert False, "Please complete your script"
```

So, for example, if you wanted to access the **Your E-Mail Address** field in the default form, you might use the expression `fields['replyto']` in your script. `replyto` is the ID or "short name" of the field in question; to find the other short names, go to the **Contents** tab of your form, click a field, and take a look at everything after the last slash in your browser's address bar. If your browser has a status bar, you can often get the same information merely by hovering over a field on the **Contents** tab—no clicking necessary.

Combining form actions

By no means are you limited to a single action adapter. In fact, it's common to stack them up. For example, a call-for-papers form for an academic conference might use the default mailer adapter to send submissions to the selection committee, but what if someone joins the committee halfway through the process? If a save data adapter was also applied to the form, the new member could easily download all the old submissions, without having to solicit a flurry of email from the others.

Another common pattern is to use two save data adapters. In situations where data is periodically downloaded from the form and processed in a different system, one save data adapter is cleared after each download in order to avoid inadvertent duplication. Meanwhile, the other accumulates submissions forever and functions as a backup.

PloneFormGen versus Archetypes content objects

When should you use PloneFormGen, and when should you develop a custom content type and use Plone's built-in edit form generation? They each have their pros and cons.

Use PloneFormGen when...

- Frequent additions or revisions of forms are required. Those needing the forms will appreciate not having to wait for development resources, and your developers will be spared the interruption. Also, you won't have to orchestrate a restart of Zope for changes to take effect.
- Data will be collected and socked away somewhere, without being called up and edited through the Web later. As seen under *Saving Submissions in the ZODB*, PloneFormGen doesn't provide much of a viewing or editing interface for saved data.

Use an honest-to-goodness Archetypes content type when...

- The collected information must be processed, reorganized, searched, or made available to other users while it's stored on your site—it's not just making a one-way trip into a copy of Excel at someone's desk. There's no easier way to collect data than with PloneFormGen, but it doesn't result in the self-contained, full-featured objects with individual workflow, sharing permissions, and all of Plone's other goodies (though see the *Filling out content objects* recipe later for a tempting hybrid approach).

Tasty recipes

PloneFormGen is an insanely flexible product. Here are a few ideas to get you started customizing it.

Testing

Simple online testing is a breeze with PloneFormGen:

1. Make a new form, and in the **Form Prologue**, explain to students that they can submit as many times as they like before the due time, but only the last submission will be counted.
2. Using the **Dates** tab on the form folder, set publishing and expiration dates for the test to constrain students to a prescribed test time if you like.
3. Add questions to the test by adding fields to the form. For example, a selection field displayed as a set of radio buttons makes a great multiple-choice question, and a rating-scale field is a natural choice for groups of true/false questions.
4. Add a string field called "Login Name". Make it **Hidden** and, on its **Override** tab, enter a **Default Expression** of `here/memberId`. This captures the student's login name so you know whose submissions are whose. While still on the **Override** tab, also check the **Server-Side Variable** box. This prevents HTML-savvy students from masquerading as others when submitting the form.
5. Add a save data adapter to keep the responses, and have it collect the submission time by checking its **Posting Date/Time** box. This lets you take the last submission by each student as the definitive one, even if you decide to re-sort the rows (say, by student name) in a spreadsheet.

Filling out content objects

Want the user-customizability of PloneFormGen *and* the full-featured goodness of proper content objects? With clever application of custom script adapters, you can rig a PloneFormGen form to spit out first-class Archetypes-based objects. We'll use News Items as an example.

First, create a PloneFormGen form with the same fields as a news item and a **Short Name** field for collecting an ID. Include at least the **Short Name** and **Title** fields, since those are the ones absolutely required to create a news item.

Next, add a custom script adapter that creates a news item and stores the submitted data in it. It's shockingly simple:

```
context.news.invokeFactory('News Item',
                           id=fields['short-name'],
                           title=fields['title'],
                           description=fields['description'])
```

- `context.news` finds the News folder that's included in a new Plone site (assuming there isn't another item with the ID "news" between the form and the root of the site).
- The `invokeFactory` method is then called on that folder to make the actual News Item, and all the attributes are passed along as keyword arguments (`id=this, title=that`), with their values being pulled out of the `fields` variable that gets passed into our script. The above code assumes we included Short Name, Title, and Description fields in our form.

All that's left is to make sure the adapter has the **Manager** proxy role so it can create the News Items, and *voilà*—a PloneFormGen form that prompts for news item info and then creates News Items!

This pattern comes in handy for satisfying interdepartmental politics while still keeping a sane back end: each department can maintain its own form with its own instructions, layout, and default values, but everything can go into one shared bin, allowing for shared processing.

Summary

We've barely scratched the surface of PloneFormGen's capabilities. It's rare to find a faster-to-deploy data collection tool and, with clever use of its extensibility mechanisms, it even blends smoothly into storing data in Plone's full-featured content types. No matter the size or mission of your organization, PloneFormGen is likely to be one of the big time-savers of your Plone deployment, truly a not-to-be-missed product.

8

Styling Your Site

Plone's stock configuration delivers a great deal of concrete functionality: workflow, security, tagging, and more. However, the people whom you need to win over—like your boss and the public—often form their first impressions of your site based solely on visual design. Replacing the out-of-the-box look of Plone with one tailored to your organization is thus a very important task.

Changing the overall look of a Plone site requires more than just the web designer's usual toolkit of HTML and CSS. In this chapter, we provide an introduction to the additional Zope- and Plone-specific techniques you need. We give an overview of Plone's somewhat complicated theming situation, show how to theme a site in a portable, reusable way, and demonstrate practices that strike a balance among ease, speed, and compatibility with future versions of Plone. Theming is a complex topic, and there are entire books on that topic alone, so we also give plenty of outside references in case your needs extend beyond the basic.

An overview of Plone theming

Plone **themes**, also known as **skins**, are visual designs that can be applied to a site, independent of its content. There are two main ways to create a theme: through the web and via the filesystem.

Through-the-web versus filesystem

One of the great advantages of Zope (and thus Plone) has historically been the customization power available through its web-based interface. Though there are some holes in this functionality with Plone 3 and 4, you can, for the most part, still point and click your way to a working theme. The advantages of this approach are:

- *Immediate feedback*. Iterations are simple. As a result, you're encouraged to test often, bugs turn up early, and bugs caught early are bugs solved easily.
- *Explorability*. Though the Zope Management Interface, where most theme work takes place, isn't the best-organized or friendliest environment in the world, it at least offers some semblance of navigable structure. You can find a piece of HTML or CSS you want to customize, click a button, and begin editing. There's less need to think abstractly.
- *Accessibility*. Through-the-web theming requires no access to the server's filesystem, so it is usable by people without, for example, Unix command-line experience or the ability to restart Zope.

The alternative is theming by developing add-on products, which live on the server's filesystem. The advantages of this are:

- *Better tools*. Expressing a theme as files and folders lets you use the entire ecosystem of filesystem-based development tools: proper text editors and version control systems, for example.
- *Ease of re-use*. Encapsulating a theme as a product means you can easily make use of it on more than one site, copy it from machine to machine, or share it with the world.
- *Completeness*. Some customizations can't yet be done through the Web: for example, moving the search box from the top of the page to the bottom by moving its viewlet into a different viewlet manager.

In practice, a filesystem product is usually better, with through-the-web styling used to test changes and to make emergency in-production tweaks between Zope restarts. Thus, this is where we will focus in this chapter.

A load of languages

Theming involves several special-purpose languages. Here's the rundown:

Language	Use in Theming
HTML	The old standby, Hypertext Markup Language defines the semantic structure of every page. Plone's markup sticks admirably to specifying meaning and avoids visual design. For example, its navigation bars are `<ul>`s, and its portlets (those omnipresent titled sidebars) are actually definition lists (`<dl>`s) with the title as the term and the content as the definition. Visual styling is applied almost wholly by CSS.
CSS	Cascading Stylesheets, another standard tool in the web designer's kit, apply a layer of visual design atop HTML. Because Plone's HTML so assiduously avoids visual design, we can change the look of a Plone site substantially without tampering with markup.
TAL	Most theming can be done with just CSS, but sometimes, like when adding new element to a page, only HTML changes will do. All HTML in Plone is produced by Template Attribute Language (TAL), a simple XML-based language so named because it nestles entirely within the attributes of XML tags. Like other templating languages, TAL is a more readable alternative to littering program code with bits of hard-coded markup. It is good for inserting content into a page skeleton, repeating portions of a page, and doing other simple presentation logic. More complicated logic is best done in Python modules, where you aren't limited to cramped one-liners. A good introduction to TAL is `http://docs.zope.org/zope2/zope2book/ZPT.html`.
METAL	The Macro Expansion for TAL (METAL) language helps combine bits of TAL from different templates to create a single page. `http://docs.zope.org/zope2/zope2book/ZPT.html#macros` is a good introduction.
Python	The general-purpose language Zope and Plone are written in. We will write almost no Python in this chapter, but it often does make an appearance in page templates. It has a much more prominent role in Zope 3-style theming than in Zope 2.
ZCML	Some parts of theming use the Zope 3 component architecture, a scheme for tying plugins and customizations into a large system like Plone. The Zope Component Markup Language (ZCML) is an XML-based language that specifies where to plug these in. For example, we will use ZCML to tie our theme product to a third-party package that drastically simplifies overriding some templates.
GenericSetup XML	A variety of XML mini-languages, which show up in your product's `profiles` folder. These are run by GenericSetup, Plone's installation framework, when your theme product is installed or uninstalled.

Don't let theming hold you up

Theming is complicated and can be time-consuming the first time through. Don't make the common mistake of letting it hold up work on the rest of your site. Indeed, most information-oriented work—audience analysis, the creation and input of content, information architecture decisions, and development of custom content types—can go on without much thought toward the coat of paint that will eventually go over it. (Likewise, you can change the look of your site later without having to redo all your navigation and content.)

The few elements to decide on ahead of time are...

- *Navigation.* What is your navigation strategy? Should the theme provide space for main or contextual navigation or for a search field? It can help to have your graphic designer join you for the last few minutes of each information architecture discussion to synchronize expectations. Drawing wireframes is another fast way to get everybody on the same page. For an excellent primer on strategies for organizing your site's content, see Peter Morville's *Information Architecture for the World Wide Web.*
- *CSS styles.* The style menu in Plone's built-in editor is commonly customized to suit the semantic needs of the site at hand. Decide early in the design process what styles will be needed: for example, body text, warning messages, sidebars containing supplementary material, and various levels of headings. It's not necessary to settle on a look for these styles—just to enumerate them and establish their CSS class names. After that, theme and content work can progress in parallel.

Prepare your development environment

Before we get down the business of creating a theme, make sure you have all the tools and settings in place:

1. *Run Zope in* **foreground mode**. When developing, always launch Zope using `bin/instance fg` rather than `bin/instance start`. At the cost of a little processor power, this greatly speeds development by...
    - Puting Zope into **debug mode**. This means it will notice certain changes to the product we're developing without needing to be constantly restarted. In Plone 3.3 and above, this automatically turns on the CSS and JavaScript debug modes as well (explained below).

- Printing error messages, usually hidden in the `event.log` file, to the terminal. Plone typically makes a lot of noise when it starts up; that can be ignored. But watch for errors, hidden among the innocuous `INFO` and `DEBUG` messages, when you exercise the functionality of your product.

2. *Turn on* **CSS debug mode**. With Plone 3.3 or above, you can skip this step, as it's implicitly done when you run Zope in foreground mode. In older versions of Plone, go into the ZMI, then to your Plone site, and finally to `portal_css`. There, turn on **Debug/development mode**. This will keep Plone from doing its clever caching, merging, and compression of stylesheets while you're developing them, helping ensure that you always see the latest version of your work. Without CSS debug mode, your CSS changes will take effect only when Zope is restarted.

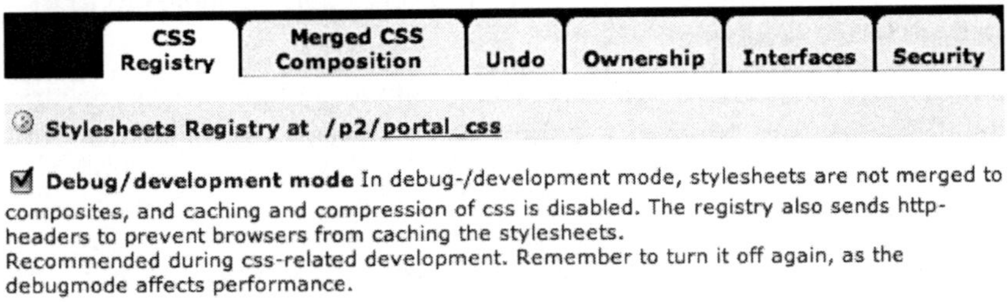

3. Get Firefox, Firebug, and the Web Developer add-on. Firefox is a nice browser, but what really makes it shine is its third-party plugins. Get the latest version, available from `http://www.getfirefox.com/`, then grab two vital plugins, Firebug (`http://getfirebug.com/`) and Web Developer (`https://addons.mozilla.org/firefox/addon/60`).
4. Turn off caching. In Firefox, show the Web Developer Toolbar (**View** → **Toolbars** → **Web Developer Toolbar**), then pull down its **Disable** menu and select **Disable Cache**. Together with enabling CSS debug mode, this will ensure that you always see your latest CSS changes. Nothing is more frustrating than spending hours chasing a problem, only to track it down to a stale cache. If you use Firefox for casual browsing, you may not wish to disable caching globally and slow down your surfing. In that case, be sure to use *Shift+Command+R* (on the Mac) or *Shift+Ctrl+R* (on other platforms) to force your stylesheets to reload when doing theme work.

Begin your theme

On-disk theme products can be quite verbose, so we employ a program to generate the skeleton of ours. We'll then make a few clean-ups before moving on to making a visual impact.

Install paster and ZopeSkel

To generate the empty shell of a theme, we'll use a code generation tool called `paster`. A set of Zope- and Plone-specific code snippets, called `ZopeSkel`, extends `paster` to provide a sort of "madlibs for Plone", churning out skeletal products whose blanks we can fill in. Here's how to get a copy of `paster` up and running:

1. Some installations of Plone come with `paster` and `ZopeSkel`; check the `bin` folder in your buildout. If `paster` is in there, you're done; skip to the next section. If not, read on.
2. Install `easy_install`, a simple Python installer, which we can use to install `paster` and `ZopeSkel`. Follow the platform-specific instructions on the `easy_install` download page: `http://pypi.python.org/pypi/setuptools`.
3. Use `easy_install` to install `ZopeSkel`, which also automatically installs `paster`. For example:

   ```
   easy_install ZopeSkel
   ```

Generate an empty theme

Once `paster` is installed, we can use it to generate an empty theme product. `paster` can generate all sorts of things, supported by various **templates**. (To see them all, type `paster create --list-templates`.) The template we're interested in is `plone3_theme`.

1. Go into the `src` folder of your buildout folder, where products under development live:

   ```
   cd your-buildout-folder/src
   ```

2. Start the process of generating a blank Plone 3 theme:

   ```
   paster create -t plone3_theme
   ```

3. `paster` needs some information to create the blank product. Answer the questions as follows:

   ```
   Selected and implied templates:
     ZopeSkel#basic_namespace  A project with a namespace package
   ```

```
  ZopeSkel#plone              A Plone project
  ZopeSkel#plone3_theme       A Theme for Plone 3.0

Enter project name: Products.PracticeTheme
Variables:
  egg:      Products.PracticeTheme
  package:  productspracticetheme
  project:  Products.PracticeTheme
Enter namespace_package (Namespace package (like plonetheme))
['plonetheme']: Products
Enter package (The package contained namespace package (like
example)) ['example']: PracticeTheme
```

The first three questions are about the name of the product. Most product names consist of two parts: a **namespace package** and the package within it. In the above example, the namespace package is `Products`, and the inner package name is `PracticeTheme`, making the product's full name `Products.PracticeTheme`.

> **Choosing a namespace package**
>
> With one exception, the choice of namespace package has no functional impact. Some people use their company name, some use `collective` to invite community contribution, and others use the default `plonetheme` to drive home the fact that this is a theme. We use the one special namespace, `Products`, because it gives us more flexibility for deployment: we can copy the inner package (`PracticeTheme`, in our case) straight into a Plone installation's `products` folder, bypassing the `buildout.cfg` configuration changes and re-running of buildout that would otherwise be necessary. The egg metadata, found in `setup.py` in the root of the generated package, is also arguably a better place than the package name for company identifiers and other semantic tags. After all, packages have been known to change ownership, and changing a package name breaks any code—and any Plone site—which uses it.

The questions continue...

```
Enter skinname (The skin selection to be added to 'portal_skins'
(like 'My Theme')) ['']: Practice Theme
```

`paster` asks for a plain-English name for our theme, which will show up in the ZMI but never be exposed to end users. Feel free to use spaces and be as wordy as you like.

```
Enter skinbase (Name of the skin selection from which the new one
will be copied) ['Plone Default']:
```

Choosing the default here (which you can do just by pressing *Return*) is always a good move. Bits of Plone's default look will then be used as fallbacks for what our skin doesn't override.

```
Enter empty_styles (Override default public stylesheets with empty
ones?) [True]: False
```

We almost always choose not to nullify Plone's out-of-the-box CSS. A typical Plone page can use upwards of 70 CSS classes, so starting from absolute scratch is a hefty commitment. Also, Plone's stylesheets are well structured and easy to build upon; they hardly ever get in the way of customizing by simple addition.

```
Enter include_doc (Include in-line documentation in generated
code?) [False]: True
```

Some commented-out documentation doesn't hurt, especially for your first few themes.

```
Enter zope2product (Are you creating a Zope 2 Product?) [True]:
```

This is always `True` for Plone, which runs on Zope 2, even though it uses some pieces from Zope 3 as well.

```
Enter version (Version) ['1.0']:
```

Choose whatever you like for a version number. Dotted sequences of numbers are typical.

```
Enter description (One-line description of the package) ['An
installable theme for Plone 3.0']:
    My first Plone theme, made for practice
Enter long_description (Multi-line description (in reST)) ['']:
Enter author (Author name) ['Plone Collective']: Erik Rose
Enter author_email (Author email) ['product-developers@lists.
plone.org']: ErikRose@ploneforeducation.com
```

Descriptions and attributions become important should you decide to distribute your theme to a large audience.

```
Enter keywords (Space-separated keywords/tags) ['web zope plone
theme']:
```

These keywords become part of your product's metadata, stored in `setup.py`. At the moment, they aren't used for much, but they might someday inform the browsing interface at the Python Package Index (`http://pypi.python.org/`). The defaults here are good and can be left alone.

```
Enter url (URL of homepage) ['http://svn.plone.org/svn/
collective/']:
```

If you are checking your theme into a version control system like Subversion—highly recommended—provide its URL here. If you distribute your theme more widely and actually create a marketing page for it, that page's URL is an even better choice.

```
Enter license_name (License name) ['GPL']:
Enter zip_safe (True/False: if the package can be distributed as a
.zip file) [False]:
```

These last two should almost always be left as they are. Plone themes must be GPL-licensed because they import from modules that are. And they must be marked as non-zip-safe because Plone doesn't use the zip-aware `pkg_resources` module to get to themes' stylesheets, templates, and images.

After you answer the last question, a large swath of text will scroll by, and you'll find a folder called `Products.PracticeTheme` deposited in your buildout's `src` folder. This, despite the fact that it comprises almost 60 files and folders, is your "blank" theme product.

4. If you are using a version control system (like Subversion), this is an excellent time to check in your theme. Its current state is, if not working exactly perfectly, at least a well-known starting point. Committing your code early will let you use your version control system to highlight any mistakes you make from this point forward. Plus, if you use descriptive commit messages and commit frequently, you'll build your own compact theming tutorial as you work.

Clean up after paster

`paster` does a fine job getting us started, but no great work of literature was ever generated from a madlibs book. We need to clean up a few messy spots of code before we get down to theming proper.

Remove redundant package registration

Because we're using the special `Products` namespace, we need to delete one line from the file `Products.PracticeTheme` → `Products` → `PracticeTheme` → `configure.zcml`. As generated, the file looks like this:

```
<configure
    xmlns="http://namespaces.zope.org/zope"
    xmlns:five="http://namespaces.zope.org/five"
    xmlns:cmf="http://namespaces.zope.org/cmf"
    i18n_domain="Products. PracticeTheme">

  <five:registerPackage package="." initialize=".initialize" />
```

```
    <include package=".browser" />
    <include file="skins.zcml" />
    <include file="profiles.zcml" />

</configure>
```

Because using the `Products` namespace gives us some registration functionality for free, we must delete the `<five:registerPackage package="." initialize=".initialize" />` line, or our product will show up twice in the **Add-on Products** control panel. It's important to do this before installing your product for the first time, or you'll have to delve into the ZMI's **Products** control panel to manually remove the errant registration.

Remove MANIFEST.in

Directly inside `Products.PracticeTheme` lives a file called `MANIFEST.in`, which specifies which files to include when building your egg. When using a version control system like Subversion that integrates with `setuptools`, Python's egg-packaging toolkit, it's best to delete this file. `setuptools` will then draw its knowledge about what to include directly from the versioning system's list of managed files and folders.

Finalize installation

Even though `Products.PracticeTheme` is in your buildout's `src` folder, Plone won't see it until you re-run buildout:

1. Edit `buildout.cfg` to enable eggtractor, a utility that lets buildout automatically see whatever is in `src`:

   ```
   [buildout]
   parts =
       zope2
       productdistros
       instance
       zopepy

   extensions = buildout.eggtractor
   ```

2. Re-run buildout.

   ```
   bin/buildout
   ```

3. Install **Practice Theme** using Plone's **Add-on Products** control panel. It should install without errors, though we haven't yet implemented any cosmetic changes.

Customize theme elements

Having generated a theme skeleton and cleaned it up a bit, you're now ready to move on to making cosmetically significant changes. These are done by overriding bits and pieces provided by Plone: CSS, images, HTML, and so on.

Let's take a look at our generated theme. Burrow into the `Products.PracticeTheme` → `Products` → `PracticeTheme` folder. (We're pretty much done with those outer folders, which provide only packaging-related boilerplate.)

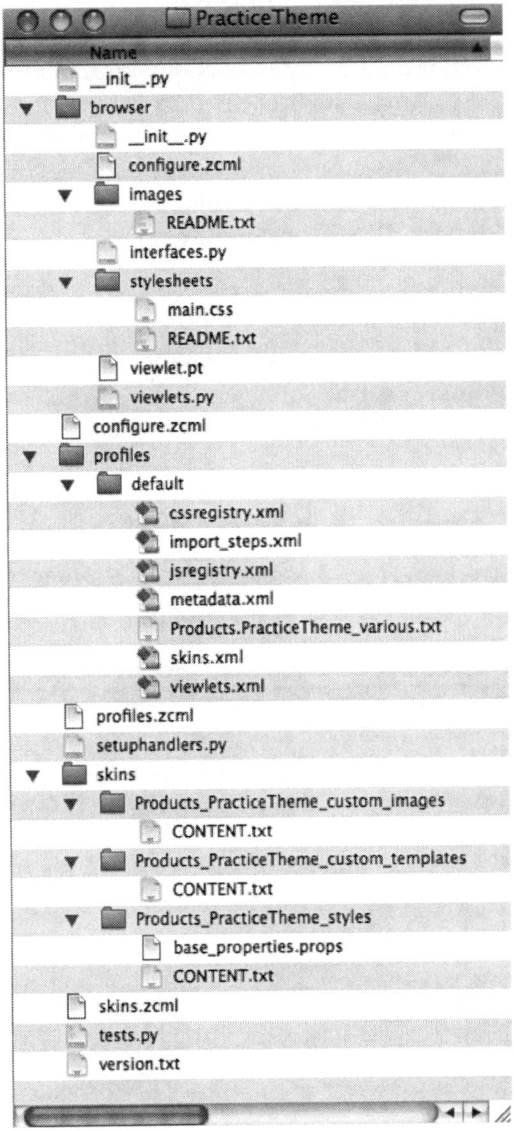

These are an awful lot of files and folders because they combine two competing and relatively independent ways of overriding theme elements:

- *The Zope 2 way*, represented by the `skins` folder. In this system, everything is mixed together in a single namespace: images, templates, stylesheets, and more: when you ask for "foo," you may get any kind of object and, because of **acquisition**, Zope's scheme for looking in many different places for an object, you may even get it from a folder that you didn't expect. As a result, the Zope 2 way is simple to learn and use but prone to name collisions, sometimes yielding surprising behavior in large deployments.
- *The Zope 3 way*, represented by the `browser` folder, swings to the other end of the spectrum. First, it does away with acquisition in favor of a more selective lookup method. Resources are identified by **interface**, which guarantees you always get the type of object you expect, not just any random object of a certain name. On the other hand, Zope 3 can feel over-engineered and tedious to work with because of its explicitness: every bit of code must be explicitly registered in ZCML configuration files.

Plone today is a mixture of these two approaches. Though Zope 2 parts are slowly being replaced with Zope 3, the expedience of the former will keep it around for a long time. As a result, we need to address both methods: Zope 2 for customizing templates, images, and other resources that are declared in the old way; and Zope 3 for customizing more recent additions.

Customize Zope 2 elements

The majority of Plone's theming machinery is built on Zope 2 and exposed though the ZMI in a tool called `portal_skins`, at the root of every Plone site.

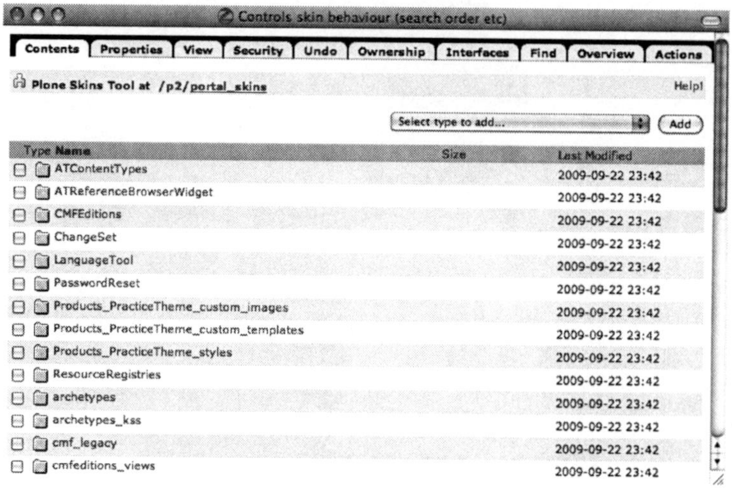

Inside `portal_skins` are folders known as **skin layers**, additional places Plone will look for things. When a theme resource is needed—for example, when an image is requested from the URL `http://example.com/plonesite/folder1/folder2/image.jpg`—Zope looks for it in the following places in a predictable order, following a scheme called **acquisition**:

- First, in `plonesite` → `folder1` → `folder2` → `image.jpg`, just as the address says. If it is not found here, Zope continues on...
- In `plonesite` → `folder1` → `image.jpg`. Zope works its way up the chain of folders (called the **acquisition chain**), looking for `image.jpg` in each.
- In `plonesite` → `image.jpg`.
- After Zope has searched the root of the Plone site, it takes a detour. It next searches each of the skin layers in order. However, it's not the alphabetical order listed on the main tab of `portal_skins`. Instead, it's the order on the **Properties** tab.

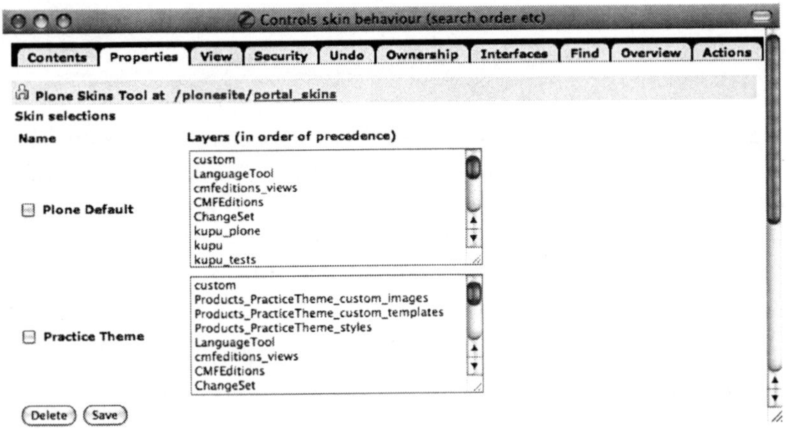

The **Properties** tab presents several alternative orderings of skin layers called **skin selections**, which, ignoring the Zope 3 side of the house for a moment, each constitute a complete theme. A skin selection can even omit skin layers whose contents it wishes to ignore.

When you install `PracticeTheme`, it adds a **Practice Theme** skin selection as shown above and makes it the default. As a result, the search order for `http://example.com/plonesite/folder1/folder2/image.jpg` becomes the following:

- As above...
  - `plonesite` → `folder1` → `folder2` → `image.jpg`
  - `plonesite` → `folder1` → `image.jpg`
  - `plonesite` → `image.jpg`

- After searching for `image.jpg` in the root of the Plone site, Zope detours into the skin layers, beginning with `custom`, the first one listed in the **Practice Theme** skin selection.
- If there is no `plonesite` → `portal_skins` → `custom` → `image.jpg`, Zope moves on to `plonesite` → `portal_skins` → `Products_PracticeTheme_custom_images` → `image.jpg`.
- ...and so on, down the list of skin layers.

Do three of these layers look familiar? `Products_PracticeTheme_custom_images`, `Products_PracticeTheme_custom_templates`, and `Products_PracticeTheme_styles` just happen to be the names of three folders in our product:

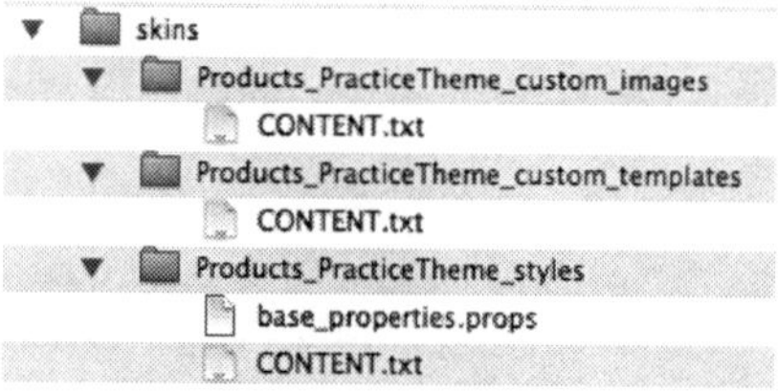

Adding images, templates, or stylesheets to their respective folders enables Plone to find them. (Actually, the names are just conventions—adding anything to any of the folders would work.) And, because `PracticeTheme`'s layers are searched before any other layers—including the ones that hold Plone's default materials—we can override anything in the default Plone distribution, simply by adding a file of the same name.

Changing images

For example, Plone's logo comes from an image called `logo.jpg`. You can see this by looking at the source code of the front page in your browser:

```
<img src="http://127.0.0.1:8080/plonesite/logo.jpg" alt=""
title="Plone" height="57" width="252">
```

To replace the stock logo with one of our own, all we need to do is add an image called `logo.jpg` to our `Products_PracticeTheme_custom_images` folder on disk. Reload the page, and you should see the new image. If you have trouble, make sure debug mode is on in `portal_css`, Zope is running in foreground mode, and your browser is not caching the old logo. (Remember: when you can't see new code, Shift-Reload!)

> **Being picky with properties**
>
> Incidentally, it doesn't matter whether the image called `logo.jpg` is actually a JPEG; neither Zope nor your web browser cares if file extensions lie. If your moral sense is offended, take a look in the `Products_PracticeTheme_styles` → `base_properties.props` file. Change the line `logoName:string=logo.jpg` to have whatever file name you wish: for example, `logoName:string=hamsterdance.gif`. Many other small style tweaks can also be made through this file, and you can substitute the values it provides into your own stylesheets (see *Changing CSS* below). Finally, the third-party CSS Manager product provides an in-Plone interface for tweaking these values, complete with proper color pickers for the non-hexidecimally inclined.

This same technique works for replacing other images and for adding new ones, which you can call in using CSS or custom HTML.

Changing CSS

Plone excels at keeping presentational elements out of its HTML, so most theming work takes place through CSS. Most of Plone's default stylesheets are found in `portal_skins` → `plone_styles`.

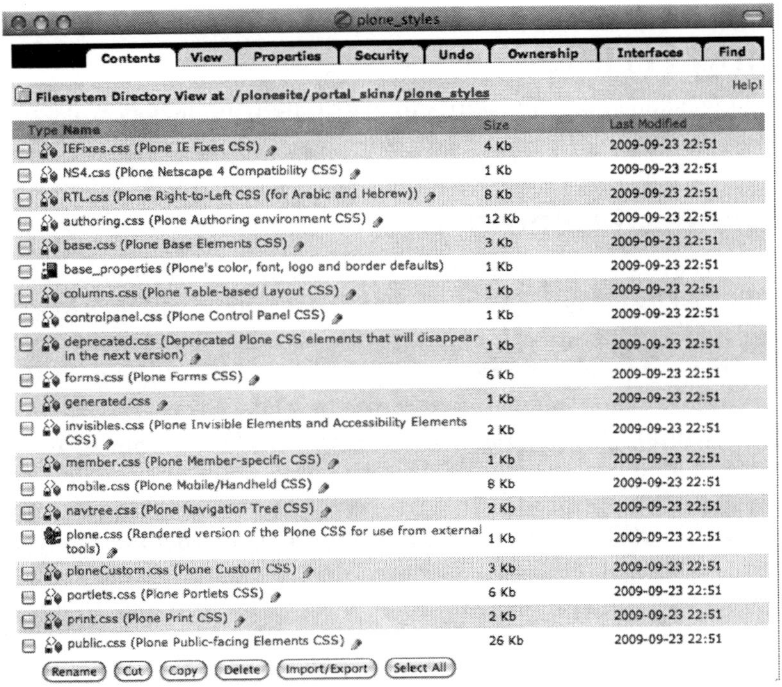

To provide the best chance for painless upgrades, it's best to avoid overriding most of these stylesheets. However, there is one special sheet whose sole purpose is to receive your modifications: `ploneCustom.css`. Here's how to set up a copy of it in your product:

1. Copy the contents of `ploneCustom.css`.
2. Paste it into the file `Products_PracticeTheme_styles` → `ploneCustom.css.dtml`. (Notice the .dtml extension; this allows the obsolete-for-5-years DTML language to substitute `base_properties` values into your CSS.)
3. Amidst a huge swath of commented-out documentation, you'll see a line urging `/* DELETE THIS LINE AND PUT YOUR CUSTOM STUFF HERE */`. Who are we to argue? For example, to change the background color of Plone's pages to a light gray, you might insert this:

```
/* DELETE THIS LINE AND PUT YOUR CUSTOM STUFF HERE */
body {
    background-color: #eeeeee;
}
```

Plone provides a wealth of CSS classes, giving you the potential for very granular control. In case Firebug is too cramped to examine the default definitions, you can find most of them in `portal_skins` → `plone_styles` →`public.css`.

Changing HTML

When CSS changes fall short, the Template Attribute Language (TAL) comes to the rescue.

The motivation behind TAL

HTML in Plone is produced by **page templates**, HTML documents interwoven with bits of the TAL language. TAL is akin to PHP's Smarty or Perl's Mason, specifically geared to generating HTML or XML documents. It lets us conditionally omit or repeat pieces of markup, insert computed content, and even do elementary computations inline. Unlike many other templating languages, TAL directives live exclusively within XML attributes in the special `tal:` namespace, meaning that a page template remains a valid XML document. Thus, a template can be edited with a WSIWYG editor like Dreamweaver without wrecking its embedded logic: good editors will skip right over (but preserve) constructions like `<p tal:condition="should_show">`. Also, because TAL and XML are such good friends, TAL makes it difficult to create an invalid XML document: things like escaping reserved characters are handled automatically.

An excellent introduction to TAL is available at `http://docs.zope.org/zope2/zope2book/ZPT.html`, with a more compact reference at `http://docs.zope.org/zope2/zope2book/AppendixC.html`.

Adding templates

Templates are added just like images and CSS: drop them into the `Products_PracticeTheme_custom_templates` folder in your product and, if you want to override an existing one, just give it the same name. For example, to make the Location field display on news item pages…

1. Find the original news item page template so you can replace it:
    - In the ZMI within your Plone site, go into `portal_types` → `News Item`.

    - Note the value of the **Default view method** field: `newsitem_view`. This is the name of the template we are looking for. (`newsitem_view` follows the typical naming convention for Zope-2-style views: `document_view` is the default template for the Document type, `event_view` is for the Event type, and so on.)

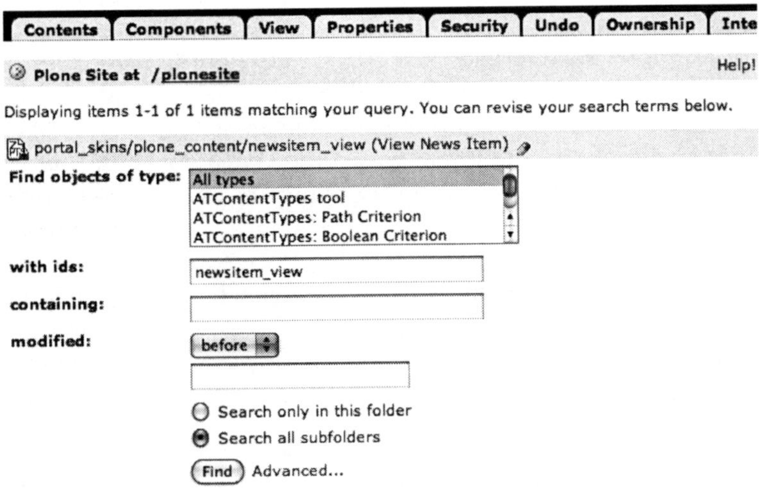

    - Still within the ZMI, navigate to the root of the Plone site, and click the **Find** tab. Search for objects with the ID `newsitem_view`.

2. Once you find `newsitem_view`, copy its contents and, using your text editor, paste them into a new file at `Products_PracticeTheme_custom_templates` → `newsitem_view.pt`. Objects in the ZMI know their types implicitly, but on the filesystem, they need a corresponding extension. In this case, the extension `.pt` stands for "page template".
3. Add the highlighted paragraph to the new file...

```
<p tal:condition="here/getLocation">
    Location: <span tal:replace="here/
getLocation">Location field of the news item will be substituted
here.</span>
</p>
<p tal:condition="python: not len_text and is_editable"
   i18n:translate="no_body_text"
   class="discreet">
    This item does not have any body text, click the edit
tab to change it.
</p>
```

Customize Zope 3 elements

Zope 3 downplays simple acquisition in favor of a more selective lookup system. Rather than having resources pulled from potentially any folder or skin layer in the acquisition chain, a Zope 3 view applies only to objects that implement a certain **interface**. As in other systems, Zope's interfaces represent a guarantee of a set of a behaviors. For example, the interface `IBaseObject` (where "I" stands for "interface") is **implemented by** objects that *provide basic Plone object behavior*, like having a title and an ID. One could write a view and register it against `IBaseObject`, and it would be usable with any object providing that basic Plone behavior. You could surf to `plonesite/some-object/@@our-view` (appending `/@@view-name` being how you explicitly ask to see a certain view) and see, for instance, a readout of title and ID. A more specific interface, like `IATNewsItem` ("Interface Archetypes News Item"), would limit the view to working only with news items. If you registered a view against `IATNewsItem` but tried to visit `plone/some-non-news-item/@@the-view`, you would get an error. To see what interfaces are implemented by an object, use the ZMI's **Interfaces** tab.

The Zope 3 method is usually more work than Zope 2. It requires explicit registration of things, where, in Zope 2, we would just drop them in a folder. It requires an understanding of abstract concepts like interfaces. Finally, in an attempt to enable recombination of software components, it often requires editing several files to make one conceptual change.

So, if this is a simple introduction to theming, why bother with Zope 3 at all? Only because we must. Some parts of Plone's pages are wired up with Zope 2 and others with Zope 3, and each must be overridden using the machinery appropriate to it. A comprehensive explanation of Zope 3 theming would fill an entire book on its own, and, in fact, several are available and cited at the end of this chapter. Here we will cover one very common use case, generalizable to the overriding of any Zope 3-registered template. If you have more advanced needs, see the end of the chapter for recommended reading.

Example: Customizing the footer

A very frequent request is to change the footer that appears on almost every page. Out of the box, it reads like an advertisement for Plone:

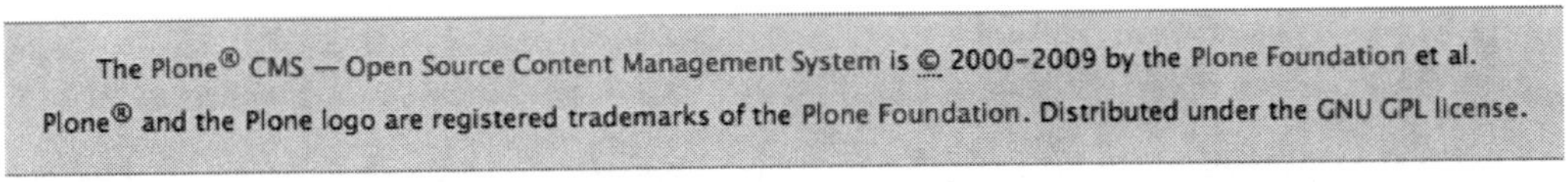

In order to replace it with more pertinent information about your own organization, we need to take two major steps.

Step 1: Set up z3c.jbot

Raw Zope 3 theming requires famliarity with abstractions like interfaces and ZCML registrations—overkill for the simple case of replacing a template. So instead, we bring in a third-party package that makes this common use case much simpler: `z3c.jbot`. "jbot" stands for "just a bunch of templates," which is all we will have to provide once it's in place. It reduces the complex Zope 3 theming story to one resembling Zope 2: create a folder, fill it with templates, and the templates of certain names will (roughly) replace the stock templates of the same names. First, however, we need to declare our theme's dependency on `jbot`:

1. In `Products.PracticeTheme` → `setup.py`, insert `z3c.jbot` into the list of packages on which `PracticeTheme` depends:

   ```
   install_requires=[
       'setuptools',
       # -*- Extra requirements: -*-
       'z3c.jbot'
   ],
   ```

   The above will cause `jbot` to be downloaded and made available to Plone the next time we run buildout. In fact, this is great time to run it.

2. Run buildout to download `z3c.jbot` and make it available to your Zope instance:

   ```
   bin/buildout
   ```

   We've made Plone aware of `jbot`. Now we need to tell our product to make use of it.

3. In `Products.PracticeTheme` → `configure.zcml`, add the highlighted lines to make it look like the following:

   ```
   <configure
       xmlns="http://namespaces.zope.org/zope"
       xmlns:five="http://namespaces.zope.org/five"
       xmlns:cmf="http://namespaces.zope.org/cmf"
       xmlns:browser="http://namespaces.zope.org/browser"
       i18n_domain="Products.PracticeTheme">

       <include package=".browser" />
       <include file="skins.zcml" />
       <include file="profiles.zcml" />
       <include package="z3c.jbot" file="meta.zcml" />
       <browser:jbot directory="templates" layer=".browser.
   interfaces.IThemeSpecific" />

   </configure>
   ```

   Here's what those three lines do:

`xmlns:browser="http://namespaces.zope.org/browser"`	Declare that this file uses the `browser` XML namespace. This makes the reference to `browser:` in the third line work.
`<include package="z3c.jbot" file="meta.zcml" />`	Another supporting line for line number three, this gives `jbot` the opportunity to make the `jbot` part of the `browser:jbot` directive work.
`<browser:jbot directory="templates" layer=".browser.interfaces.IThemeSpecific" />`	This line does the actual magic. It tells `jbot` to look in the `Products.PracticeTheme` → `Products` → `PracticeTheme` → `templates` folder and override Plone's stock templates with what it finds. The `layer=".browser.interfaces.IThemeSpecific"` part specifies that the found templates should take effect only in Plone sites where our theme is installed.

4. Our next step is to create the `templates` folder we told `jbot` to expect. Create an empty folder at `Products.PracticeTheme` → `Products` → `PracticeTheme` → `templates`.

Step 2: Override templates

All that's left is to put a properly-titled file in our new `templates` folder and add our desired footer markup to it. However, to determine the proper title, we'll need to take a bit of a winding road through several management pages.

Plone's pages are made up of small pieces of HTML called **viewlets**, of which the footer is one. Our first order of business is to find out what the footer's viewlet is called.

1. In your Plone site, go to any page that shows the original footer, like the site's front page.
2. Add `/@@manage-viewlets` to the end of the URL, yielding something like `http://127.0.0.1:8080/plone/@@manage-viewlets`, and go to that page.
3. This new page shows an exploded view of the page you were just on, broken down by viewlet. Scroll to the bottom of the page, and note that the label above the footer reads `plone.footer`.

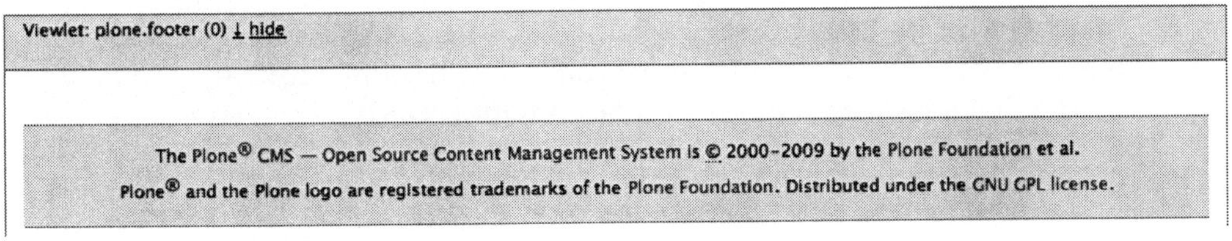

4. Keeping that label in mind, navigate to your Plone site in the ZMI, then to `portal_view_customizations`. This is a list of all templates that must be customized using Zope 3 techniques.

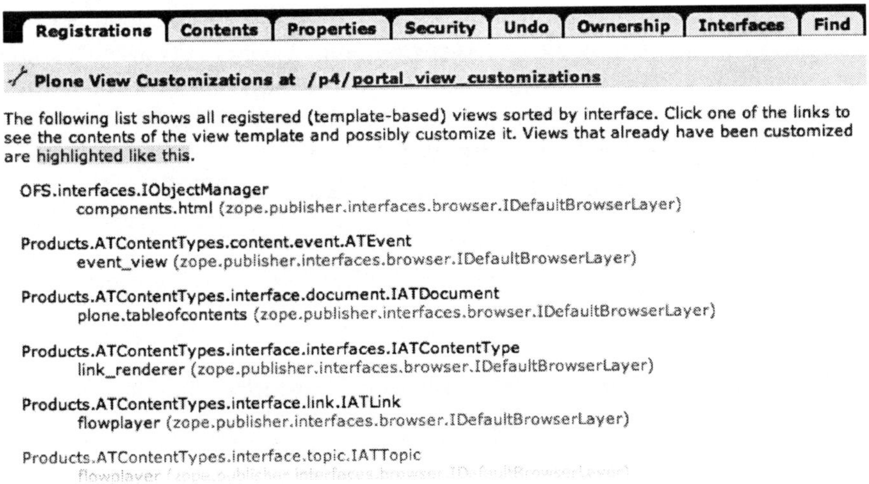

5. Search for `plone.footer`, and click it.You'll be greeted with some technical information about the view and its current implementation.

view name
plone.footer
registered for interface
zope.interface.Interface
registered for request type
zope.publisher.interfaces.browser.IDefaultBrowserLayer
template file
plone.app.layout.viewlets/footer.pt
zcml file
plone.app.layout.viewlets/configure.zcml

```
<div id="portal-footer" metal:define-macro="portal_footer" i18n:domain="plone">

<p>
    <span i18n:translate="description_copyright" tal:omit-tag="">
    The
    <span i18n:name="plonecms" tal:omit-tag="">
        <a href="http://plone.org" i18n:translate="label_plone_cms">Plone<sup>&reg;</
    </span>
    is
    <acronym title="Copyright" i18n:name="copyright" i18n:attributes="title title_cop
```

6. Make note of the path `plone.app.layout.viewlets/footer.pt` under **template file**. This is what we must call our overriding footer template, except that the slashes must be replaced with periods.

> **Customizing views through the Web**
>
> Incidentally, at this point, you could scroll all the way to the bottom of the page, click the **Customize** button, and override the template using a web-based interface. Your changes wouldn't become part of your product, but sometimes this approach is expedient.

7. In `Products.PracticeTheme` → `Products` → `PracticeTheme` → templates, create a new file called `plone.app.layout.viewlets.footer.pt`, and fill it with your footer content. The markup you saw above in Step 5 makes a good starting point; copy and paste it so you don't have to start from scratch. A very simple final result might be...

```
<div id="portal-footer" metal:define-macro="portal_footer">
    <p>
        Copyright 2010 My School
    </p>
</div>
```

8. When you are ready to test your new footer, restart Zope. Plone's footer should show your new copyright message.

Further Reading

Zope 3 theming is powerful but difficult to learn, and many hundreds of pages have been written on the topic. Some good printed materials include...

- *Plone 3 Theming*, by Veda Williams
- Chapters 17 and 18 of *Practical Plone 3*—over 100 pages combined

Many online tutorials and references are also available:

- `http://plone.org/documentation/phc_topic_area?topic=Visual+Design`
- `http://weblion.psu.edu/wiki/UserInterfaceDevelopment`

Finally, if you get stuck, there's always the `#plone` IRC channel on `irc.freenode.net`, full of people happy to lend a hand.

Summary

In this chapter you have...

- Seen how Plone mixes Zope 2 and Zope 3 approaches and become familiar with the basics of each
- Built the skeleton of a theme product
- Learned how to customize CSS, images, and HTML for Zope 2 elements
- Seen how to override templates registered using Zope 3 methods

9
Going Live

Up to now, you may have had Plone installed on a staging server to let your content contributors collaborate. Its performance may even seem acceptable if traffic is low. But exposing a simple Plone installation to a larger audience would deliver a slow, insecure experience for everyone.

Plone's rich feature set means that it does a lot of work on each request: checking security on every involved object, walking along the acquisition chain, and rendering TAL templates. As a result, delivering a snappy experience on a popular site would seem to require a large investment in high-end hardware. In addition, Zope doesn't speak HTTPS on its own, so any passwords would be passed unencrypted, vulnerable to anyone in the right place with a packet sniffer.

To solve these problems, a production Plone setup adds a smorgasbord of different server processes, each offering some element of security or scalability to throw into the pot. At the end, a delicious Plone stew emerges, ample to feed the big, hungry crowds of the Internet.

Introducing the stack

This chapter is a tour through the setup of a single robust Plone server. Very large sites might need to spread across a cluster of machines, but the single-server configuration herein will suffice for 95% of deployments. As a guideline to whether you're in that 95%, here are some approximate performance metrics we're aiming for:

- 800 anonymous requests per second (of cached content)
- 40 authenticated requests per second

As always, premature optimization causes premature thinning of the hair, so, unless the web statistics from your old site show a strong need for more, start with a single server. It's easy to expand later.

The earlier numbers are within easy reach of relatively modest commodity hardware: for example, two 2.4-GHz, dual-core Xeons and 8 GB RAM. Plone will happily eat all the processor you can provide, performance scaling fairly linearly with CPU speed. RAM is the second most important consideration—and cheap—so don't skimp on that either.

The basic service stack looks like this:

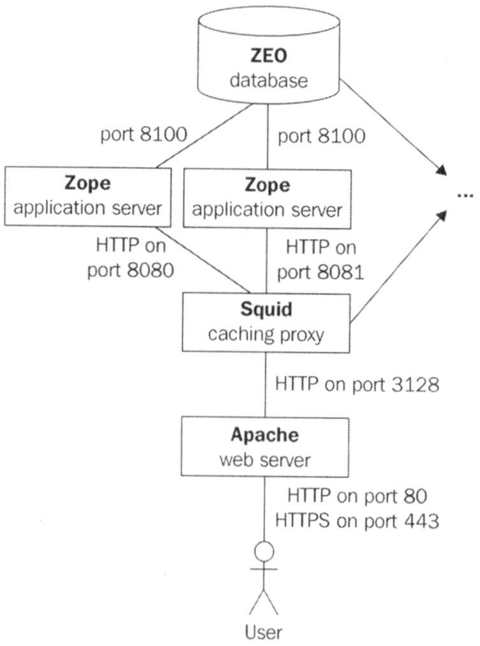

A rough explanation of the above:

- ZEO, which stands for Zope Enterprise Objects, is a specialized database for storing Python objects. ZEO takes over Zope's job of reading from and writing to `Data.fs` files and instead offers the database to Zope over a socket. This lets us run multiple copies of Zope against the same data and split the web-serving workload among them. We will look deeper into ZEO momentarily.

- Squid acts as an HTTP **reverse proxy**, which means that it accepts web requests from Apache, forwards them along to Zope, and then passes Zope's response back in the other direction. In the process, it caches stylesheets, images, and pages so Zope doesn't waste its time computing the same things over and over. Squid also does simple load balancing among the multiple Zopes.
- Finally, Apache faces the user and handles HTTPS, virtual hosting, and, optionally, authentication and redirections.

A word about platforms

Our recommended stack of servers can run well on both Windows and Unix-like operating systems, and most of the instructions in this chapter will work on either. For those who want a recommendation, the Stable release of Debian Linux provides first-class quality control, nearly hands-free updates, and great Python support. Having deployed on the Mac, Windows, and several Linux flavors, the author has suffered the least long-term pain from Debian. Some command-line examples in this chapter are thus targeted at Debian—but, aside from minor syntactical differences, they should work on any platform. Also, while some Debian-specific package names are mentioned, comparable packages are available for practically all Unix-like operating systems (try MacPorts on the Mac), and installers for Windows are just a Google away.

When using Debian, what release should I choose?

Debian has a 3-tier release process: Unstable, Testing, and Stable. But don't be put off by the naming; even Testing is about as reliable as a typical Red Hat release. Official releases of software first enter the Unstable tier (or **distribution**), where they get vetted by thousands of users who like to live on the edge. After a package has been in Unstable for ten days without any serious bugs reported, it makes its way into Testing. Stable then harvests the contents of Testing about once every year and a half.

Stable is a good choice if all you need are Squid and Apache—that is, if you aren't using your Plone server for a lot of other tasks as well. Stable gets no updates except for security patches, so you never have to worry about the behavior of software changing behind your back, and you never have to revise your config files due to incompatible upgrades.

If you find you need newer software than Stable provides, Testing is also fine in practice, as long as you can take five minutes of downtime per week for updates and don't mind answering occasional prompts about config file updates. If you're uncertain about your ability to troubleshoot in a Linux environment, it's safest to stick with Stable.

A more Windows-like experience

Servers like Apache and Squid, though they claim first-class support for Windows, do retain a bit of Unix flavor, making Windows-only administrators feel a bit out of place. A commercial product called Enfold Proxy, available for a few hundred dollars, makes this all go away. Enfold Proxy integrates with Microsoft's IIS through a custom ISAPI filter and handles caching and load balancing in place of Squid. Meanwhile, IIS handles the front-end web service, obviating the need for Apache. Setup is a point-and-click breeze, and support is fantastic, making Enfold an easy recommendation if you have a strong need to deploy on Windows.

ZEO and Zope

With an operating system chosen, we can move on to learning about and configuring the first two layers of the stack, Zope itself and the ZEO database server.

A typical desktop installation of Plone involves a single Zope process, which reads from and writes to a `Data.fs` file directly. ZEO, Zope's specialized database server, takes over that responsibility, and one or more copies of Zope (called **Zope instances**) communicate with it via a socket. This setup has several advantages:

- *Scalability*. ZEO's main benefit is the ability to run more than one Zope instance at a time on a single data set. Python takes poor advantage of multiple or multi-core processors, and their ubiquity in today's hardware makes this a prime optimization even for single-server deployments. A good rule of thumb is one Zope instance for every logical processor; for example, if you have a single dual-core processor, run two Zopes. Don't worry about leaving a core free for ZEO or other parts of the stack; Zope is the only CPU-hungry process. If you reach the limits of a single server (after the caching and other optimizations described in the following sections), add more Zope instances on additional servers.

Python's multiprocessor problem

Python's poor use of multiple processors is a common point of complaint. The immediate cause is the Global Interpreter Lock (**GIL**), which keeps any two threads of a Python program from executing interpreted code at once. Such a coarse lock simplifies both the interpreter and any machine-language extension modules. And in theory, it shouldn't inhibit multiprocessor use much, at least in programs which spend most of their time in C library code, since the lock is generally released when venturing into C. However, Plone spends much of its time in CPU-heavy interpreted code like template rendering. This causes the lock to be held quite often, making the trade-off less appealing.

Attempts have been made to replace the GIL with a collection of finer-grained locks, but the overhead of acquiring and releasing the additional locks made for an unclear advantage in practice. Guido van Rossum, the language's Benevolent Dictator For Life, has no plans for further efforts to remove the GIL and recommends a multi-process—rather than a multithreaded—approach to parallel processing. This is what ZEO enables.

- *Reliability*. With more than one Zope instance in play, an important reliability feature pokes its head out. Do you need to restart a copy of Zope for a product upgrade? Go ahead. With load balancing set up, another instance will field its requests. (Technically, there could be race conditions: data formats in new versions of products could conflict with the old ones for the few seconds they coexist. However, these are practically unheard-of in practice.)
- *Debuggability*. With an instance-independent data store, you can debug your production site without bringing down the service. Just run `bin/instance debug`, and examine your site from an interactive Python interpreter. (It's a common misconception that you need a dedicated Zope instance just for running `debug`. As long as you're using ZEO, it's perfectly safe to use one that's already running.)
- *Maintenance*. Database packing, a routine disk-space-saving task discussed in the next chapter, is easier to automate in a ZEO environment.

Considering buildout

The most future-proof way to construct and maintain a cluster of Zope instances is with **buildout**, a sort of hybrid package manager and build system. If you have ever installed Plone 3.2 or greater, you used buildout to do it—though it may have been hiding behind a graphical installer. Buildout performs a slew of installation-related tasks: it computes dependencies, downloads the packages that comprise Plone, assembles Zope and ZEO instances, and puts their configuration in place. It can also be extended to do other arbitrary tasks, though we will stay fairly conservative.

> **How far to push buildout**
>
> Buildout can be extended with arbitrary Python **recipes** to do just about anything. There are recipes for building and setting up Apache and Squid (or the new kid on the block, Varnish) and even for building a dedicated copy of Python. However, going this far is just a needless repetition of the packaging and quality assurance efforts of a good Linux distribution—only with a much smaller bug-reporting populace and fewer development resources. Thus, this chapter uses buildout for Zope and ZEO only and relies on operating system packages for the remainder.
>
> Conversely, Plone packages are sometimes available for popular Linux distributions, but they are almost universally out of date. Until Plone 3.2, Debian had excellent Plone packages, but the technical challenges of an egg-based distribution, along with political pressures, have ended support for the foreseeable future.

Buildout takes its instructions—what software to install and how to configure it—from a config file called `buildout.cfg`. Since the file is long, we will once again use the code generation tool `paster`, along with its accompanying set of Zope blueprints, ZopeSkel, to generate a first draft.

Install the generator, and generate a buildout configuration

The installation process for `paster` and ZopeSkel is a bit convoluted if you aren't already accustomed to using `easy_install`, but generating a `buildout.cfg` this way does give you the best chance for future compatibility. Here's the process, from the ground up:

1. ZopeSkel requires Python. If you don't already have Python 2.4 installed, grab a copy. (Be sure not to stray beyond Python 2.4.x, as 2.5 and up won't work with Plone until version 4.) For example, in Debian Linux 5.0, installing Python is as simple as...

   ```
   sudo aptitude install python2.4
   ```

2. Install `easy_install`, a simpler Python installer than buildout, in order to install ZopeSkel and `paster`. Follow the instructions at its download page according to your platform: `http://pypi.python.org/pypi/setuptools`.
3. Use `easy_install` to install ZopeSkel, and `paster` automatically comes along with it. For example, on Debian...

   ```
   sudo python2.4 /usr/bin/easy_install ZopeSkel
   ```

4. Navigate to wherever you'd like to install Plone, and ask `paster` for a copy of the `plone3_buildout` template. (You can see other available templates by typing `paster create --list-templates`.)

   ```
   cd /var/lib/plone
   sudo paster create -t plone3_buildout plone
   ```

`paster` will make a `plone` folder in the current directory and drop a `buildout.cfg` inside that contains your answers to its questions. Here are some reasonable answers.

```
Selected and implied templates:
  ZopeSkel#plone3_buildout  A buildout for Plone 3 projects

Variables:
  egg:      plone
  package:  plone
  project:  plone
Enter plone_version (Which Plone version to install) ['3.3.2']: 3.3.1
Enter zope2_install (Path to Zope 2 installation; leave blank to fetch
one) ['']:
Enter plone_products_install (Path to directory containing Plone
products; leave blank to fetch one) ['']:
Enter zope_user (Zope root admin user) ['admin']:
Enter zope_password (Zope root admin password) ['']: my_funky_password
Enter http_port (HTTP port) [8080]:
Enter debug_mode (Should debug mode be "on" or "off"?) ['off']:
Enter verbose_security (Should verbose security be "on" or "off"?)
['off']:
```

For most of the above, just press *Return* to use the value between the brackets. All we really need to fill out is the Plone version and the administrator password.

You should get a `plone` directory containing, among other things, a `buildout.cfg` file. Open that and you'll find the following, which we will explain below:

```
[buildout]
parts =
    zope2
    productdistros
    instance
    zopepy

# Change the number here to change the version of Plone being used
extends =
    http://dist.plone.org/release/3.3.1/versions.cfg
versions = versions


# Add additional egg download sources here. dist.plone.org contains
archives
# of Plone packages.
find-links =
    http://dist.plone.org/release/3.3.1
    http://dist.plone.org/thirdparty

# Add additional eggs here
eggs =

# Reference any eggs you are developing here, one per line
# e.g.: develop = src/my.package
develop =
[versions]
# Version pins for new style products go here
plone.recipe.zope2instance = 3.6



[zope2]
# For more information on this step and configuration options see:
# http://pypi.python.org/pypi/plone.recipe.zope2install
recipe = plone.recipe.zope2install
fake-zope-eggs = true
url = ${versions:zope2-url}

# Use this section to download additional old-style products.
# List any number of URLs for product tarballs under URLs (separate
```

```
# with whitespace, or break over several lines, with subsequent lines
# indented). If any archives contain several products inside a top-
level
# directory, list the archive file name (i.e. the last part of the
URL,
# normally with a .tar.gz suffix or similar) under 'nested-packages'.
# If any archives extract to a product directory with a version
suffix, list
# the archive name under 'version-suffix-packages'.
[productdistros]
# For more information on this step and configuration options see:
# http://pypi.python.org/pypi/plone.recipe.distros
recipe = plone.recipe.distros
urls =
nested-packages =
version-suffix-packages =

[instance]
# For more information on this step and configuration options see:
# http://pypi.python.org/pypi/plone.recipe.zope2instance
recipe = plone.recipe.zope2instance
zope2-location = ${zope2:location}
user = admin:admin
http-address = 8080
#debug-mode = on
#verbose-security = on
# If you want Zope to know about any additional eggs, list them here.
# This should include any development eggs you listed in develop-eggs
above,
# e.g. eggs = Plone my.package
eggs =
    Plone
    ${buildout:eggs}

# If you want to register ZCML slugs for any packages, list them here.
# e.g. zcml = my.package my.other.package
zcml =

products =
    ${buildout:directory}/products
    ${productdistros:location}

[zopepy]
# For more information on this step and configuration options see:
# http://pypi.python.org/pypi/zc.recipe.egg
```

```
recipe = zc.recipe.egg
eggs = ${instance:eggs}
interpreter = zopepy
extra-paths = ${zope2:location}/lib/python
scripts = zopepy
```

Make your first buildout tweaks

A `buildout.cfg` is made of bracketed sections containing parameters and values, like a Windows `.ini` file:

```
[some_section]
some_parameter = some_value
```

A parameter can also have more than one value, if the values are split up onto multiple lines and indented:

```
[some_section]
some_parameter_with_multiple_values =
    one
    two
    three
```

Finally, comments are preceded by hash marks:

```
# This is a buildout comment.
```

As an opening tweak, let's make sure our Zope instances run as securely as possible. First, they should run as the `plone` user rather than the almighty `root`. In the unlikely case that Plone goes awry or is commandeered through a security hole, this will keep it confined to its own directory rather than stomping all over the rest of the disk. To configure this, add an `effective-user` parameter under the `[instance]` section:

```
[instance]
# For more information on this step and configuration options see:
# http://pypi.python.org/pypi/plone.recipe.zope2instance
recipe = plone.recipe.zope2instance
effective-user = plone
zope2-location = ${zope2:location}
```

We'll make a similar addition in the next section to safeguard ZEO as well.

Next, tell Zope to listen only on the loopback interface. This will keep people from connecting directly to it from other machines, bypassing the security and optimizations provided by the rest of our server stack. Add `localhost:` to the `http-address` parameter:

```
[instance]
# For more information on this step and configuration options see:
# http://pypi.python.org/pypi/plone.recipe.zope2instance
recipe = plone.recipe.zope2instance
#effective-user = plone
zope2-location = ${zope2:location}
user = admin:admin
http-address = localhost:8080
```

Add ZEO support to buildout.cfg

Next, add ZEO support and a second Zope instance. You can add more instances later following the same pattern. (As mentioned earlier, one Zope per core is a good rule of thumb.) In the very first section, add `zeoserver` to the `parts` parameter:

```
[buildout]
parts =
    zope2
    productdistros
    instance
    zopepy
    zeoserver
```

This tells buildout to look for the `[zeoserver]` section we're about to create. Next, add this section at the bottom of the file:

```
[zeoserver]
recipe = plone.recipe.zope2zeoserver
zope2-location = ${zope2:location}
zeo-address = localhost:8100
effective-user = plone
```

This tells buildout to make a ZEO instance that listens on port 8100, listens only to requests coming from the local machine, and runs as the user `plone`.

We already have one Zope instance out of the box, but we need to tell it to use ZEO for its data storage needs. To configure this, add `zeo-client` and `zeo-address` parameters to the `[instance]` section:

```
[instance]
# For more information on this step and configuration options see:
# http://pypi.python.org/pypi/plone.recipe.zope2instance
recipe = plone.recipe.zope2instance
zope2-location = ${zope2:location}
user = admin:my_funky_password
http-address = localhost:8080
#debug-mode = on
#verbose-security = on
zeo-client = on
zeo-address = localhost:8100
```

Next, add a second Zope instance at the bottom of the file. We'll use the `collective.recipe.zope2cluster` recipe, which lets us essentially clone our first instance and change just the listening port:

```
[instance2]
recipe = collective.recipe.zope2cluster
instance-clone = instance
# We need only specify what differs from the first instance:
http-address = localhost:8081
```

If you have more than two processor cores, add more instances until you have one for each. All that needs to change on new ones is the section name (`[instance3]`, for example) and the `http-address`.

Finding buildout documentation

Each buildout recipe has a plethora of configuration options, many more than shown here. Most recipes keep their documentation at PyPI. Just take the recipe name, and tack `http://pypi.python.org/pypi/` onto the front. For example, details on the `collective.recipe.zope2cluster` recipe are at `http://pypi.python.org/pypi/collective.recipe.zope2cluster`.

Finally, add a pointer at the top of your buildout to the `[instance2]` section (and any other instances you have added), like so:

```
[buildout]
parts =
    zope2
    productdistros
```

```
instance
instance2
zopepy
zeoserver
```

This tells buildout to pay attention to the other sections; any section not listed is ignored.

Add CacheFu to the buildout

The next piece in our deployment puzzle is a quartet of products collectively called CacheFu. Their function is twofold:

1. Do a bit of caching within the Zope process
2. Advise the downstream Squid cache—which we will explore momentarily—how long to cache things for, by setting various HTTP response headers based on a configurable set of rules

Thus, our last `buildout.cfg` tweak is to add CacheFu. Add the highlighted line to the bottom of the `[instance]` section, making it look like the following:

```
[instance]
# For more information on this step and configuration options see:
# http://pypi.python.org/pypi/plone.recipe.zope2instance
recipe = plone.recipe.zope2instance
zope2-location = ${zope2:location}
user = admin:my_funky_password
http-address = localhost:8080
#debug-mode = on
#verbose-security = on
zeo-client = on
zeo-address = localhost:8100

# If you want Zope to know about any additional eggs, list them here.
# This should include any development eggs you listed in develop-eggs
above,
# e.g. eggs = Plone my.package
eggs =
    Plone
    ${buildout:eggs}
    Products.CacheSetup
```

"CacheSetup" is the name of the top-level product that ties the other members of the CacheFu quartet together. The other three are pulled in automatically as dependencies.

Start it up

Now that buildout is configured, run it, and it will download and install ZEO and Zope.

1. Run `bootstrap.py` with your copy of Python 2.4 to initialize your buildout setup. This only needs to be done once.

   ```
   python2.4 bootstrap.py
   ```

2. Then run buildout, which downloads and installs everything:

   ```
   bin/buildout
   ```

> **Oh no! Something has gone wrong!**
>
> While buildout is eminently flexible and the canonical way of installing Plone these days, it does have certain shortcomings. Aside from syntax errors in `buildout.cfg`, the most common errors stem from its dependency on the network. Out of the box, buildout contacts several different servers in the course of installing Plone. If any of these is down (which they occasionally are) or someone has uploaded a buggy package (which they occasionally do), your buildout may grind to a premature halt and spit out an error message in the form of a Python traceback. If you are comfortable reading the error and it looks like a connection problem, your best bet is to wait a few hours and try again. Otherwise, sign onto the Plone chat room at `http://plone.org/support/chat`, and ask if anyone else is having similar problems; typically, errors due to buggy uploads or downed servers are widespread, and you will receive a quick reply.
>
> One error of special note is the spurious `SyntaxError: 'return' outside function`. These are actually normal and should be ignored. For the curious, they happen because the installation step which pre-compiles `.py` files into `.pyc` ones cannot distinguish between proper Python modules and `.py` files containing Zope's through-the-web Script (Python) objects, which have slightly different syntax.

3. Once everything has completed successfully, start up ZEO:

   ```
   bin/zeoserver start
   ```

   Then, start each Zope instance:

   ```
   bin/instance start
   bin/instance2 start
   ```

To bring the servers up and down on startup and shutdown, arrange to run the above commands (and their `stop` equivalents) automatically. For example, on Debian, symlink them into `/etc/init.d/` and manage them like typical init scripts:

```
ln -s /var/lib/plone/bin/zeoserver /etc/init.d/zeoserver
ln -s /var/lib/plone/bin/instance /etc/init.d/zope1
ln -s /var/lib/plone/bin/instance2 /etc/init.d/zope2
```

In case you don't already have a favorite way of managing init scripts, the `sysv-rc-conf` tool, available after first running a quick `sudo aptitude install sysv-rc-conf`, saves a lot of typing. On a Debian machine, run `sysv-rc-conf`, then tell Zope and ZEO to start under runlevels 2, 3, 4, and 5, like so:

```
┌ SysV Runlevel Config   -: stop  =/+: start h: help  q: quit ┐
|
|
| service      1      2      3      4      5      0      6
S        |
| ------------------------------------------------------------
---------- |
| zeoserver   [ ]    [X]    [X]    [X]    [X]    [ ]    [ ]
[ ]        |
| zope1       [ ]    [X]    [X]    [X]    [X]    [ ]    [ ]
[ ]        |
| zope2       [ ]    [X]    [X]    [X]    [X]    [ ]    [ ]
[ ]        |
```

Increase speed with caching

Plone's feature-richness makes it heavy on the CPU. To reach our targets for real-world performance, we add a few layers that remember the computed renderings of pages and avoid redoing all the work each time. This approach is managed by two layers:

1. Squid, which works as a caching HTTP reverse proxy, remembering the contents of rendered pages, images, and files for as long as their HTTP headers advise (or until explicitly told to stop)
2. CacheFu, an in-Plone tool that sets those headers according to a complex set of rules

Crank up CacheFu

Caching is often a balancing act between speed and staleness: how long can you afford to serve a page that may be out of date? CacheFu ships with very conservative settings, which yield no staleness and give about a 400% speed boost, measured by requests per second on an unauthenticated front page. These stock settings neither assume—nor take advantage of—a caching proxy like Squid.

Our first task is to correct this. We'll move some of the caching out of the Zope process—as in-Zope caching still costs it considerable thinking for each request—and into Squid, which is written in efficient C and has power to spare.

1. In your Plone site, head to **Site Setup → Add-on Products**, and install CacheSetup, which we earlier downloaded and put in place using buildout. (The other three CacheFu products don't need explicit installation through the Web.)
2. Under **Site Setup**, visit the **Cache Configuration Tool**, which will appear under the **Add-on Product Configuration** heading.
3. Configure the following settings:

Enable CacheFu	On
Active Cache Policy	**With Caching Proxy**
Proxy Cache Purge Configuration	**Purge with VHM URLs**

Site Domains	`http://mysite.example.edu:80`
	`https://mysite.example.edu:443`
	Replace these with your actual domain names, of course. Include any other domains you'll be serving as well, each on its own line. Be sure to include a port number for each.

Proxy Cache Domains	`http://127.0.0.1:3128` If you ever add more servers to your farm, this should always point to the one running Squid (assuming you choose to share a cache among the machines).
Compression	**Never**. We'll handle this in Apache to save even more Zope cycles.
Vary Header	Empty this, since Apache, not Zope, will worry about whether the browser can accept compressed content.

The page should look like this:

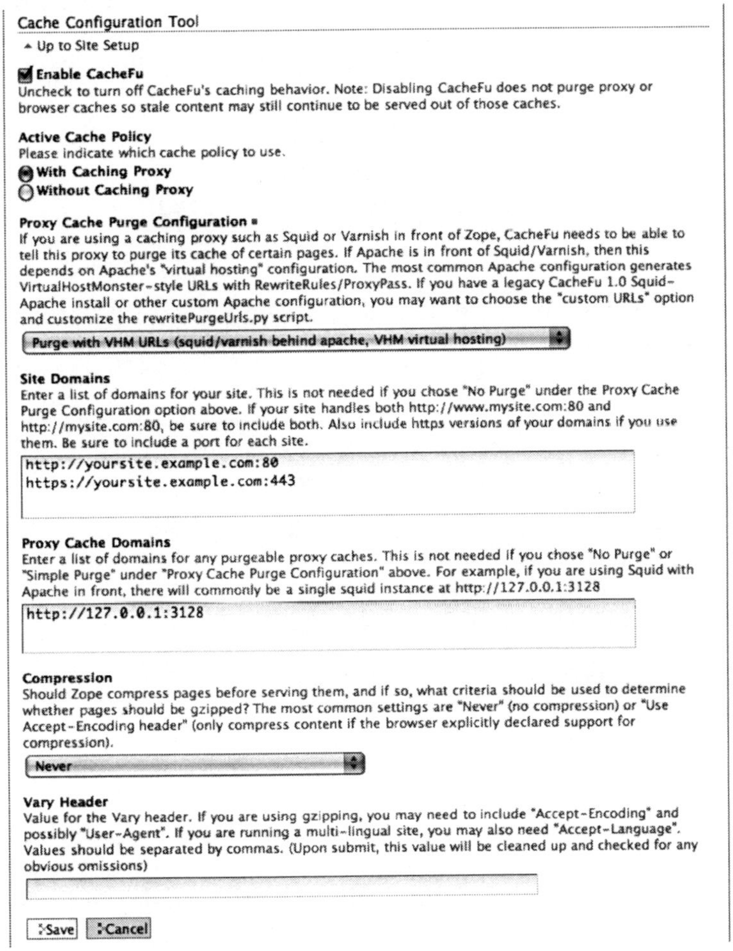

Now that we have the basic settings in place, we can tweak the rules by which CacheFu decides where and how long to cache various content:

1. Visit the **Rules** tab, and click the **Content** ruleset. This rule determines how to cache non-container types like pages and news items. (The **Rules** tab is a bit buggy in Safari. If the link doesn't take you anywhere, use your browser's contextual menu to copy its address and paste it into the address bar.)

2. Set **Header Set for Anonymous Users** to **Cache in proxy cache for 24 hours**. CacheFu is smart enough to notice when non-container (**non-folderish**) items change and to purge old copies from Squid's cache in response. Thus, we can cache these types of pages in Squid essentially essentially without a time limit.

3. While you're at it, under **Content Types**, select any third-party non-folderish types you've added.

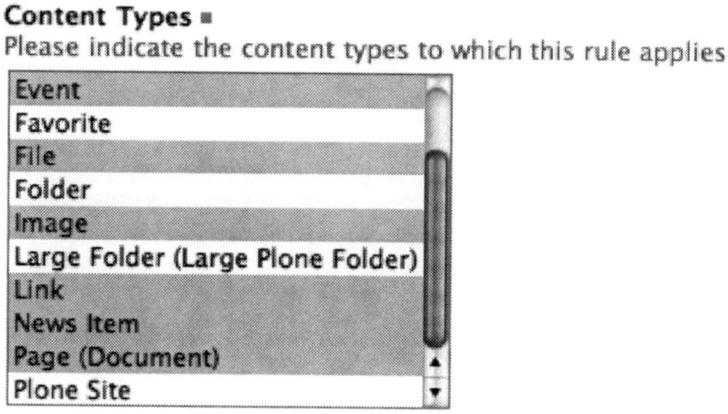

Caching folderish items is trickier. CacheFu's automatic purging works by hooking the catalog's `reindex` method and purging several known views of any object that changes. Therefore, it works reliably only on pages that depend solely on the object pointed to by the page's URL (that is, the published object). For example, the rendering of a folder listing depends not only on the folder object itself but on the items within it (and sometimes even the items within those). Playing it safe and purging all the parent folders of a changed item would drag performance into the gutter. A conservative configuration would thus preserve CacheFu's default behavior for container types: caching everything within the Zope process, where it is immune from staleness. However, if you are willing to trade a few minutes of staleness for a better chance at surviving sudden bursts of high traffic, you can cache containers in Squid for just a few minutes. Then, if you receive 200 requests a second for an hour or two, unauthenticated visitors might get folder listings a few minutes old, but at least they'll get something instead of a timeout.

CacheFu's shortest cache-in-proxy period out of the box is one hour, which is too long for a visitor to receive a stale folder view. So, we first need to add the option to cache for only a few minutes:

1. In the **Cache Configuration Tool**, head to the **Headers** tab.
2. Copy and paste to duplicate the **Cache in proxy cache for 1 hour** headerset.
3. Open it, and re-title it "Cache in proxy cache for a few minutes".
4. Scroll down the page to find the **s-maxage** header. (Don't be fooled by the subtly different **max-age** header.) Set it to 180 seconds or thereabouts. Even caching for just one minute takes an enormous load off Zope during rush periods.

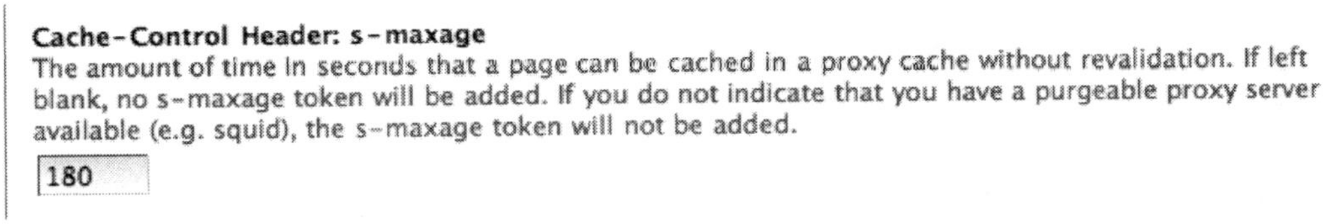

5. Click Save.
6. Under the Rules tab, open the Containers ruleset, set its **Header Set for Anonymous Users** to **Cache in proxy cache for a few minutes**, and save. Presto! Now your folderish types require only one hit to Zope every three minutes, worst case. Of course, your logged-in users will continue to see fresh results, so editing can continue unimpeded.

7. While you're in the **Containers** ruleset, select any new folderish content types you've added under **Content Types**. These should include almost all the types from Faculty/Staff Directory, for example, since the information on, say, a Person page is determined in part by the publication states of related Specialty objects.

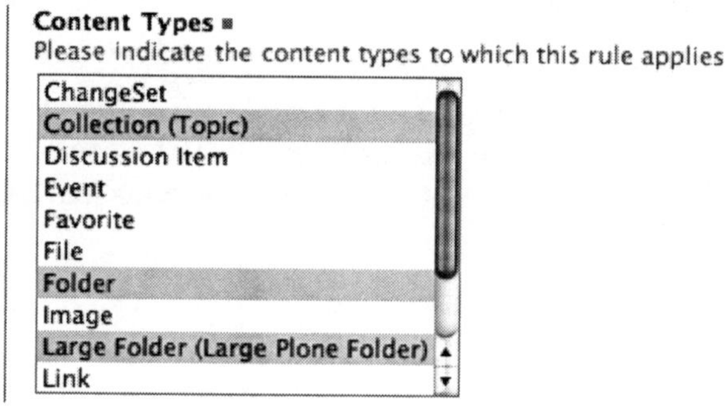

8. Remember to save.

Set up Squid

Now that Zope is running and knows how to communicate with it, it's time to actually set up Squid. Squid has a reputation of being hard to configure, but this applies more to its day job as an HTTP *forward* proxy. Since we're using it as a reverse proxy, configuration is very simple. After installing Squid 2.x, for example via an OS package…

```
aptitude install squid
```

…replace the contents of its configuration file (usually in a place like `/etc/squid/squid.conf` on Unix-like systems) with the following:

```
# This configuration file requires squid 2.6+.  It is untested with
# squid 3.x.

# Present a special hostname in error messages, etc.
# visible_hostname mysite.example.edu
# This defaults to the result of gethostname(), so no need to
# hard-code this.

# What local user gets mail if the cache dies
# cache_mgr support
# Defaults to "webmaster"

# If starting Squid as root, this will change the effective/real
```

```
# UID/GID to the user specified below.  The default is to change
# the UID to nobody.
cache_effective_user proxy
cache_effective_group proxy

# The port on which to listen:
#   "vhost" turns on accelerator mode using Host header for virtual
#      domain support
#   "defaultsite" defines the default domain to use for Host header
http_port 127.0.0.1:3128 vhost

## Squid log files
# cache_access_log /var/log/squid/access.log
# cache_log /var/log/squid/cache.log
# cache_store_log /var/log/squid/store.log
## Turn off logging; there's no sense logging what Apache already
## does.
cache_store_log none
# cache_log /dev/null
logfile_rotate 0  # This is the default for Debian, which uses
                  # logrotate.

# Set cache directory and size (5000 MB) - be sure to set the cache
# size to about 10% less than the physical space available to leave
# room for squid's swap files and other temp files
cache_dir ufs /var/spool/squid 5000 16 256

# Amount of memory used for recent objects (default: 8 MB)
cache_mem 64 MB
high_memory_warning 400 MB

# Max cached-on-disk object size (default: 4096 KB)
maximum_object_size 100 MB

# Max cached-in-memory object size (default: 8 KB)
maximum_object_size_in_memory 1 MB

# Squid requires a default 'all' acl
acl all src 0.0.0.0/0.0.0.0

# Purge access - only Zope servers can PURGE
# Doesn't really do much good when Apache is on the same IP as Zope.
# We'll stop incoming PURGEs in Apache's config.
acl zope_servers src 127.0.0.1
```

```
acl purge method PURGE
http_access allow zope_servers purge
http_access deny purge

# Zope instances configured as cache peers
cache_peer 127.0.0.1 parent 8080 0 no-query no-digest originserver
    name=instance_1 round-robin
cache_peer 127.0.0.1 parent 8081 0 no-query no-digest originserver
    name=instance_2 round-robin
# no-digest quiets log messages due to Zope not furnishing cache
# digests.

# Cache peer access
acl virtual_host_monster urlpath_regex ^/VirtualHostBase/https?/.*
cache_peer_access instance_1 allow virtual_host_monster
cache_peer_access instance_2 allow virtual_host_monster
cache_peer_access instance_1 deny all
cache_peer_access instance_2 deny all

# Don't let anybody but Apache hit us
acl localhost src 127.0.0.1/255.255.255.255
http_access allow localhost
http_access deny all

digest_generation off

# Deny caching of POST requests
acl post_requests method POST
cache deny post_requests
```

The above is based on configuration from a generator that ships with CacheFu. From that beginning, it acquired several tweaks, borne of the travails of production experience. It requires very little site-specific customization. For example, you needn't hard-code any hostnames or set any timeout parameters; everything is set through the Web in CacheFu.

The sections you should examine are two. First, there is an assumption (correct on Debian) that an unprivileged user called `proxy` exists. If it doesn't, you'll need to add one before starting Squid, by doing something like `adduser proxy`.

Second, make sure there's a `cache_peer` line and two `cache_peer_access` lines in the following section for every Zope instance you created earlier:

```
# Zope instances configured as cache peers
cache_peer 127.0.0.1 parent 8080 0 no-query no-digest originserver
name=instance_1 round-robin
cache_peer 127.0.0.1 parent 8081 0 no-query no-digest originserver
name=instance_2 round-robin
# no-digest quiets log messages due to Zope not furnishing cache
digests.

# Cache Peer Access
acl virtual_host_monster urlpath_regex ^/VirtualHostBase/https?/.*
cache_peer_access instance_1 allow virtual_host_monster
cache_peer_access instance_2 allow virtual_host_monster
cache_peer_access instance_1 deny all
cache_peer_access instance_2 deny all
```

These allow Squid to act as a lightweight load balancer, which is sufficient in most cases. Requests are distributed on a round-robin basis among your Zope instances, making use of all your processor cores. You can even stop a Zope instance to perform maintenance, and the others will pick up the slack, allowing you to do zero-downtime upgrades.

Pound, a more flexible load balancer

If you find yourself adding machines of varying capability to your server farm, you may find it worthwhile to interpose the more capable load balancer Pound between Squid and Zope; it can, for example, decide the routing of requests based on varying speeds of different machines. Of course, it is another moving part to go wrong, so we omit it in the simple case. Plenty of sites simply let Squid do the balancing.

At this point, Squid should be ready to go! Start it in whatever way is appropriate to your operating system. On Debian, for example...

```
/etc/init.d/squid start
```

Squid will create its disk cache directories and start listening for requests. To make sure it's working, run `wget http://127.0.0.1:3128/VirtualHostBase/http/mysite.example.edu:80/my-plone-site/VirtualHostRoot/` (replacing `mysite.example.edu` with your actual domain name and `my-plone-site` with the ID of your Plone site). A good-looking Plone front page should download.

On top of CacheFu's fourfold speed boost, Squid should deliver another factor of 100-200. With the two working together, you should easily be able to hit 800 requests per second even on low-end server hardware.

> **Varnish, a new reverse proxy**
>
> In the past year or so, another contender as emerged to challenge Squid. Varnish is a reverse proxy built to do nothing but caching. As a result, it delivers moderately higher performance than Squid. Though it was unreliable to the point of weekly core dumps and other erratic behavior back in version 1.1.2, it has matured greatly in its 2.x series. Intrepid administrators may wish to give it a try.

Add Apache

The Apache web server is the last piece of our service stack. Like Ruby on Rails or Tomcat, Zope has its own simple HTTP server, but fronting it with Apache gives us many additional features often necessary in a production environment:

- HTTPS support
- Virtual hosting
- Fast, regular-expression-based redirections
- Compression of responses for faster transfer
- Support for a wide ecosystem of modules providing access control, content transformation, and more

Apache is well supported in any package management system, and binaries are available for Windows (though IIS also works fine if you install a third-party filter to enable proxying). On Debian, installation is as simple as...

`aptitude install apache2`

We'll also need a few modules:

- `mod_proxy`, which provides the general framework for reverse proxying
- `mod_proxy_http`, which provides HTTP proxying in particular, using the above
- `mod_rewrite`, which lets us drive our reverse proxying with flexible regular-expression-based pattern matching
- `mod_deflate`, which compresses outgoing content so it takes less time and traffic to transfer

These modules aren't always enabled by default. On Debian, a simple `a2enmod proxy_http rewrite deflate` will enable all four. On other platforms, you might need to edit one of Apache's config files, often `httpd.conf`, and insert or uncomment lines similar to these:

```
    LoadModule proxy_module /usr/lib/apache2/modules/mod_proxy.so
    LoadModule proxy_http_module /usr/lib/apache2/modules/mod_proxy_
http.so
    LoadModule rewrite_module /usr/lib/apache2/modules/mod_rewrite.so
    LoadModule rewrite_module /usr/lib/apache2/modules/mod_deflate.so
```

Generate correct links with VirtualHostMonster

Naively forwarding requests to Squid at `127.0.0.1:3128`, which would then forward them to Plone at, for instance, `127.0.0.1:8080`, would technically work. However, for all Plone knows, it is talking to a user on the local machine. It would therefore render links in its pages as `http://127.0.0.1:8080/`..., which would make it impossible for visitors to get anywhere. To generate the right links, we combine the address of the requested content with some hints about the public-facing URL to make a specially formed address like this:

```
http://127.0.0.1:3128/VirtualHostBase/http/mysite.example.edu:80/
my-plone-site/VirtualHostRoot/
```

This URL is intercepted by a built-in Zope object called **VirtualHostMonster**, which helps Plone construct the right links. Here's a breakdown of the VirtualHostMonster URL syntax:

Syntax	Meaning
`VirtualHostBase`	A keyword that tells VirtualHostMonster to get involved.
`http/mysite.example.edu:80`	The URL scheme, hostname, and port to use for generated links. Even if you're using a default port like 80 or 443, you must still include it here explicitly.
`my-plone-site`	After the port number comes one or more path segments to traverse in Zope but omit from generated links. A Plone site's ID will appear here when hosting one Plone site per hostname.
`VirtualHostRoot`	A keyword that marks the point after which path segments will be included in generated links.
`some-folder/some-page`	Path segments included after `VirtualHostRoot/` are both traversed and added to generated links. Most of an object's path within a Plone site will appear here.
`_vh_other-segment`	Path segments after `VirtualHostRoot/` that start with `_vh_` are included in generated links but not traversed within Zope. This is rarely used but invaluable when you want to park a Plone site deep within an existing site: say, at `http://www.example.edu/engineering/electrical/the-plone-site`.

Our example URL...

```
http://127.0.0.1:3128/VirtualHostBase/http/mysite.example.edu:80/
my-plone-site/VirtualHostRoot/
```

...asks for the front page of the Plone site `my-plone-site`. It tells Plone to render links as if the site is served from `mysite.example.edu` via `http` on port `80`. `my-plone-site` is not to be included in generated links.

VirtualHostMonster URLs like these are generated by the Apache configuration in the next section.

A sample Apache configuration

Apache configurations are always a major point of customization; no one configuration can pretend to cover all or even most deployments. Fortunately, Apache's documentation, available at `http://httpd.apache.org/docs/`, is excellent. To get you started, here is a simple virtual host that maps requests on the `mysite.example.edu` domain to their corresponding locations inside the Plone site called `my-plone-site`. Be sure to read the explanatory comments before each directive.

```
# Always use the value of the ServerName directive, not the incoming
# Host header, when determining the value of the SERVER_NAME variable:
UseCanonicalName On

<IfModule mod_deflate.c>
    # Compress HTML, text, XML, and CSS. Leave JavaScript alone,
    # because IE versions 5.5-7 have bugs in their decompression.
    #
    # On Debian, /etc/apache2/mods-enabled/deflate.conf is a better
    # place for this configuration.
    AddOutputFilterByType DEFLATE text/html text/plain text/xml text/
css
</IfModule>

<VirtualHost *:80>
    # Make this VirtualHost block respond when the Host header is
    # mysite.example.edu (or if the Host header is missing and this is
    # the first VirtualHost Apache encounters while reading its config
    # files):
    ServerName mysite.example.edu

    ServerAdmin webmaster@mysite.example.edu

    # Even if serving multiple named virtual hosts on one machine, I
    # find that one gigantic, shared log file is most convenient for
    # analysis. However, you can also break them up into individual
    # logs by changing the file name below:
    CustomLog /var/log/apache2/access.log combined

    # Some distributions of Apache, including Debian's and Red Hat's,
    # have very conservative default settings which prevent all
    # proxying, even the very safe reverse proxying we're doing.
    # Lighten up; you're safe unless you set ProxyRequests to On.
    <Proxy *>
        Order deny,allow
```

```
        Allow from all
    </Proxy>


    # Turn mod_rewrite on:
    RewriteEngine On

    # Forbid users from sending PURGE requests through Apache to
    # Squid. There are plenty of better denial-of-service attacks on
    # Plone, but this is one fewer:
    RewriteCond %{REQUEST_METHOD} ^PURGE
    RewriteRule .* - [F]

    # If you have other custom configuration--more RewriteRules or the
    # like--this is a good place for them.

    # For URLs with a trailing slash, strip the slash before passing
    # it through to Squid. If we didn't do this, Squid might also
    # encounter a request for the URL without the slash and cache two
    # copies, pointlessly wasting space and halving the cache hit
    # ratio. Note that, in normal operation, Plone doesn't generate
    # any URLs with trailing slashes.
    RewriteRule ^(/.*)/$ $1

    # Turn the requested URL into a VirtualHostMonster URL, and
    # forward the result along to Squid (and, ultimately, Zope):
    RewriteRule ^/(.*) http://127.0.0.1:3128/VirtualHostBase/
http/%{HTTP_HOST}:80/my-plone-site/VirtualHostRoot/$1 [L,P]
</VirtualHost>
```

Summary

In this chapter, we've assembled and configured all the pieces of a production Plone stack: multiple Zopes taking advantage of all available processors, Squid and CacheFu saving Zope from redoing work, and Apache tying it all together with some virtual hosting and bandwidth-saving compression. With these pieces in place, you can be confident of a request rate of over 800 cached anonymous hits per second, along with 40 authenticated hits per second for each of your Zope instances. Read on to the next chapter to learn how to keep it all up to date and operating smoothly.

10
Maintenance, Backups, and Upgrades

Once you have a production-quality Plone site up and running, there are a few routine tasks that will keep it running smoothly. And, if your server should ever unexpectedly become a smoking hole in the ground, it's nice to have reliable backups on hand. This chapter shows how to do the periodic tasks that will keep you out of trouble; give your users a smooth, uninterrupted experience; and keep Plone and your add-on products up to date.

Pack the ZODB

The first of the periodic maintenance tasks is packing the Zope database.

Why to pack

First, a little background.

Zope's object database, **ZODB**, is one of its most compelling features. Automatically translating Plone's Python objects to on-disk representations, the ZODB divests developers of a whole layer of concerns they would otherwise have to spend time on: for example, setting up an object-relational mapping layer like SQLAlchemy.

Out of the box, the ZODB stores its contents in the `Data.fs` files you may have seen lurking in the `var` folders of your Zope instances. `Data.fs` files rarely travel alone. More often, they hang out with their friends: `Data.fs.index`, `Data.fs.tmp`, and a few others. Here's a who's-who of the `Data.fs` crew:

`Data.fs`	This is where the important data lives: all your pages, folders, images, and even your Site Setup settings. Though the head of the gang, `Data.fs` files are really just simple lists of transactions. ZODB transactions—which are just like transactions in any other database product—usually have a one-to-one correspondence to HTTP requests. Each transaction starts with a header, followed by a storage-suitable—or **pickled**—representation of the objects changed during the request: 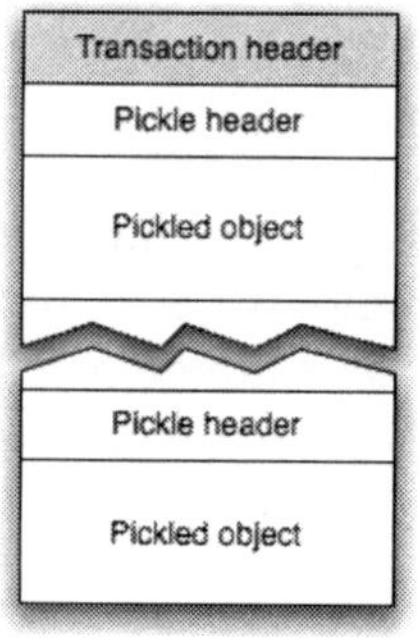 The ZODB only ever tacks new transactions onto the end of the file; it never goes back and modifies previous ones.
`Data.fs.old`	Created as an artifact of the packing process, which we'll discuss momentarily, `Data.fs.old` contains the same data as `Data.fs` did before it was packed. In fact, it is actually the untouched, old `Data.fs` file renamed.
`Data.fs.index`	Since `Data.fs` is just a chronological list of changes to objects, it would take an awfully long time to start at the end and scan backwards every time Zope needed the latest revision of an object. `Data.fs.index` is a performance optimization, a continually updated record of where the latest version of each object is in the `Data.fs`. Also, because it's just a shortcut, `Data.fs.index` is expendable: if you delete it, it will be automatically recreated the next time Zope or ZEO starts up.

`Data.fs.lock`	A "pidfile", for the Unix-heads in the house. When ZEO starts up, it creates this file and puts its process ID number inside. This acts as a sort of bookmark to keep you from accidentally starting two copies of ZEO at once using the same `Data.fs`—which could easily lead to data loss. When ZEO shuts down, this file is deleted. If ZEO crashes—a basically unheard-of event—this file will be left behind. Be careful to confirm that the process referred to by its contents is no longer running; only then should you delete the file so ZEO will start back up.
`Data.fs.tmp`	An artifact of ZODB's two-phase commit implementation, this contains only the last committed transaction—and then only for a moment, until the second phase of the commit completes. It's not important to back up.

As hinted above, a `Data.fs` is like a book chiseled in stone tablets: you can always add more to the end, but you can never change what has already been written. One capitalization on this design decision is the **Undo** tab in the ZMI: because old transactions are preserved, you can remove a series of recent ones to essentially go back in time. (Note that this is different from Plone's **History** tab, which works using higher-level data structures and is not affected by packing.) A less desirable consequence of the stone-and-chisel approach is that the `Data.fs` grows continually as more recent revisions of objects are added, while old revisions, representing outdated copies of objects, hang around and take up space. This stone book gets very heavy after awhile! But never fear: "packing" is a maintenance procedure that solves this problem.

Packing keeps your `Data.fs` slim by throwing away revisions of objects that are out-of-date or that are no longer referenced by other objects. (The ZODB is organized as a single-rooted hierarchy; if an object can't be reached from the top of the tree, then no one will ever see it, and there's no point keeping it around.) Theoretically, one could pack the ZODB by throwing away any object revisions that are unneeded as of *right now*. However, there are certain pathological cases where corruption might occur if a revision is in use by a transaction that's also going on *right now*. So, in practice, a grace period is used. For example, throwing away any non-current revisions older than seven days is often a reasonable trade-off between file size and maintaining the ability to undo.

While a large `Data.fs` carries no innate performance penalty (unless stored on a fragmentation-prone filesystem like NTFS), it does take up space and can make backups cumbersome, depending on your backup strategy. Upon packing, a new copy of the `Data.fs` is generated containing only relatively current data, the old file is renamed to `Data.fs.old`, and the database uses the new file from that point forward. Incidentally, Zope can continue serving requests as usual during a pack. Because the ZODB uses a low-interference locking model called **multiversion concurrency control** and because packing is a logically read-only operation, the action never has to stop.

> **On alternative storages**
>
> There are several alternative ways for the ZODB to store its content behind the scenes. While the interface presented to Zope and add-on products doesn't change, there are a variety of pluggable **storages** that can be selected by a system administrator. The default, FileStorage, stores objects in the familiar `Data.fs` files—where "fs" stands for "FileStorage". Other popular choices—though easily under five percent of total production installations—include RelStorage, which stores everything in a separate relational database, and DirectoryStorage, which represents everything as files and folders on the filesystem. The answers to the most obvious followup questions are all "no": no, RelStorage doesn't make the database schema amenable to querying in a useful way; no, DirectoryStorage doesn't yield files that can be opened with any off-the-shelf program; and no, using an alternative storage doesn't exempt you from having to pack the database (though RelStorage's history-free option does reduce the need). The alternative storages have some performance characteristics that are useful in special situations, but the out-of-the-box FileStorage, combined with ZEO, is the best choice in almost all cases. Conveniently, FileStorage also has ease of setup on its side, along with the thorough testing and wide support that come from its being the default.

Pack manually

This is only for special occasions—for instance, reducing the weight of a `Data.fs` before moving it to a new machine. You can pack the ZODB manually by visiting Zope's database management interface through the web:

1. From Plone, go to **Site Setup → Zope Management Interface → Control_Panel → Database Management**.

This lists the ZODB databases available to Zope: by default, a `main` one, where all the important information lives, and `temporary`, which holds almost exclusively sessioning information, held only while a user remains logged in. (Note that any relational databases you are using won't show up here; they don't need to be packed but should rather be maintained according to their own database product's documentation.) `temporary`, as its name implies, gets cleared when Zope stops, so, unless you manually add more databases—a technique unnecessary for the vast majority of sites—`main` is the only one you have to pack.

2. Click the `main` database.

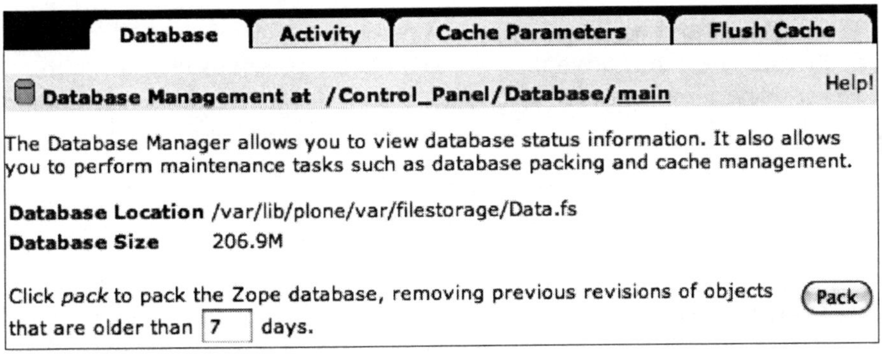

3. Put 7 into the **days** field. This will clear out obsolete objects older than a week.
4. Click **Pack**.

Pack automatically

So that you don't have to keep coming back and manually clicking buttons, you should schedule packs to happen automatically every so often. A common schedule is to pack weekly and discard unused object revisions that are over seven days old. This means you can still use the ZMI's undo functionality to time-travel backwards between one and two weeks at any given time while still keeping your hard drives from brimming over. To do this, we take advantage of the server operating system's built-in scheduling features. On a Unix-like operating system like Debian Linux, we can use the `cron` utility.

There are a couple of ways to initiate a pack. One often cited in how-tos is to programmatically emulate the clicks we made in the above section using a web fetcher like `wget` or `curl`. This usually involves hard-coding passwords into a script and also depends on the format of the form, which could conceivably change. A better way is to call the `zeopack` utility—automatically inserted in your buildout's `bin` folder—which talks directly to the ZEO server.

Schedule easily with /etc/cron.weekly

If your operating system has an `/etc/cron.weekly` folder (as Debian does), your task is easy:

1. Put the following into a file called `pack_zodb` (or whatever descriptive title you like) within `/etc/cron.weekly`, and it will run every week, typically around 6:47 a.m. on Sunday. (If you're curious, check `/etc/crontab` for the exact time.)

   ```
   #!/bin/sh
   /var/lib/plone/bin/zeopack -h 127.0.0.1 -p 8100 -d 7
   ```

   The arguments to `zeopack` in your script tell it to connect to ZEO on port 8100 (following the convention we used in the previous chapter) and remove any unused revisions of objects older than 7 days. The above assumes your buildout folder is at `/var/lib/plone`; adjust the script as necessary.
2. Make your `pack_zodb` script executable so `cron` will be able to run it:

   ```
   chmod a+x /etc/cron.weekly/pack_zodb
   ```

Schedule manually

If you use a Unix-like operating system but it doesn't provide the convenience of an `/etc/cron.weekly` folder, just use the `crontab` command to set up the recurring task. It's a few more steps, but you get more control, being able to choose the exact time the pack happens:

1. Decide when to pack. Unless you collect so much data in a week that you overflow your disk, once a week will suffice. Every Sunday morning during the wee hours is usually a safe bet, or you can examine your past web statistics to more quantitatively determine a low-traffic time. However, beyond creating some work for your storage devices, packing doesn't interfere with users' experience, so don't worry too much about the schedule unless you run a heavily loaded server.
2. With `cron`, each system user has its own list of associated periodic tasks. If you've made a dedicated user under which to run Zope—which is a good idea—that user's task list (or **crontab**) is a good place to keep the daily pack. First, become that user. For instance, if the user is called "zope"...

   ```
   su zope
   ```
3. Next, edit the crontab:

   ```
   crontab -e
   ```

This brings up a (possibly empty) list of periodic tasks, one per line. Each line begins with of a series of numeric fields (sometimes populated by asterisks) that control when the task begins. The line ends with the command that actually performs the work. If a commented-out list of column headings isn't already at the top of the crontab, you may want to insert it for your own sanity:

```
# minute  hour  day-of-month  month  day-of-week  command
```

4. Take the time you decided in step 1, and translate it into the column-based format `cron` understands. For a weekly task like this, you need to specify the day of the week as well as the time of day. To pack at 6:47 a.m. on Sundays, for instance, put this into the crontab:

```
# minute  hour  day-of-month  month  day-of-week  command
  47      6     *                   *      0
```

   The asterisks simply mean "do the task no matter the value of this column". For example, the asterisk under "month" means "Pack the database no matter what month it is". Under the "day-of-week" column, 0 represents Sunday, 1 is Monday, and so on.

5. Finally, add the command that actually does the packing, under the `command` column. The final crontab should look like this:

```
# minute  hour  day-of-month  month  day-of-week  command
  47      6     *                   *      0            /var/lib/plone/
bin/zeopack -h 127.0.0.1 -p 8100 -d 7
```

   You may recognize this command from the `cron.weekly` steps above. Again, this configuration assumes your buildout folder is at `/var/lib/plone`; adjust it as necessary.

Pack early and often

Remember that packing works by copying the useful information out of the current `Data.fs` and into a new one. The old `Data.fs` is renamed to `Data.fs.old` but otherwise kept unmolested; thus, packing a database can, at worst, use up to once again the amount of disk space as the original `Data.fs`. If you're short on storage, be sure to pack frequently, before the database gets so large that you don't have room to accommodate the `Data.fs.old` and the newly packed `Data.fs`.

Back up Plone

For the most part, a simple filesystem-level backup of your buildout folder (that it, is the one housing `buildout.cfg`) is all that's necessary. Your add-on products, `buildout.cfg`, Zope and ZEO instances, log files—all are conveniently centralized in that folder, so including it in your normal backup routine will almost completely suffice. What remains is to ensure a reliable backup of the ZODB: like many databases, it requires some special care to copy it while it is running.

Make incremental backups of the ZODB with repozo

Of course, it would be possible to shut down ZEO, copy the `Data.fs` to a backup medium, and then start everything back up again, but your site would be unavailable while you did it. `repozo`, a tool included in your buildout's `bin` directory, does incremental backups of `Data.fs` files while they're in use, avoiding downtime. It also brings the following advantages over the simple stop-everything-and-copy method:

- Backs up only what's changed since the last backup, saving the wasted I/O of retransmitting gigabytes of unchanged transactions each time. This also makes it feasible to do smaller backups much more often.
- Supports point-in-time restores to any backup, all without keeping a bunch of redundant, multi-gigabyte `Data.fs` files around.
- Transparently compresses backups, usually to about 25% of their original size.

However, an interaction with packing adds a small complication. `repozo` works by taking advantage of the stone-tablet property of `Data.fs` files: it never needs to reexamine a transaction after it's been backed up once. However, when a `Data.fs` is packed, some transactions are discarded, and the rest shift around to fill in the holes. This forces `repozo` to start from scratch. Thus, the first `repozo` backup after a pack is necessarily a full backup, even if you ask for an incremental one.

Make repozo easier to use

It's perfectly alright to call `repozo` directly from `cron`, but instead, we'll take a moment to wrap it in a layer of sugary goodness known as `collective.recipe.backup`. This is an add-on to your buildout that provides backup and restore scripts even easier to use than `repozo` alone. Here's what it gives you, above and beyond raw `repozo`:

- The ability to say simply "`backup`" and "`restore`" rather than "`repozo -BvzQ -r /var/lib/plone/var/backup -f /var/lib/plone/var/filestorage/Data.fs`"
- Automatic deletion of old incremental backups. Historically, it's been each administrator's responsibility to script a way to get rid of them, lest they fill up your backup drive. By default, the `backup` script keeps the current and previous full backups and discards earlier ones, along with their incrementals.
- A handy snapshotting capability that lets you take a copy of a production `Data.fs` on demand—for testing on a staging server, for instance—without interfering with the server's normal backup schedule. See the documentation for more on this: `http://pypi.python.org/pypi/collective.recipe.backup#snapshots`.

Here's how to install `collective.recipe.backup`:

1. Shut down Zope and ZEO, and make a quick copy of your buildout folder (the one with `buildout.cfg` in it), just in case our upcoming run of buildout destroys the universe. (It shouldn't, but, as buildout relies on many projects with varying levels of quality control, it can be unpredictable.) Leave out the bulky `var/filestorage` folder; buildout has no chance of trashing your `Data.fs`.
2. Add `collective.recipe.backup` to `buildout.cfg`:

```
[buildout]
parts =
    ...other existing parts...
    backup

[backup]
recipe = collective.recipe.backup
```

3. Then, run `bin/buildout -N` to download and run the new recipe. (`-N` keeps buildout from trying to update Plone itself or your products in the process; we don't want any trouble. In the latest versions of Plone, `-N` is the default behavior.) Your buildout folder will receive several additions:
   - `bin/backup` and `bin/restore` scripts to run
   - `var/backup` and `var/snapshotbackup` folders for backups to land in

Schedule nightly backups

Now that the easy-to-use backup and restore scripts are in place, we can schedule nightly backups, again using `cron`. If your operating system has an `/etc/cron.daily` folder (which Debian does), just follow these steps:

1. Put the following into a file called "`back_up_zodb`" (or whatever descriptive title you like) within `/etc/cron.daily`, and it will run every night:

   ```
   #!/bin/sh
   /var/lib/plone/bin/backup --quiet
   ```

   (The above assumes your buildout folder is at `/var/lib/plone`; adjust the script if that's not the case.)
2. Make your `back_up_zodb` script executable so `cron` will be able to run it:

   ```
   chmod a+x /etc/cron.daily/back_up_zodb
   ```

If your operating system does not have a `cron.daily` folder, use the same technique described above under *Schedule manually*.

> **Backing up more often**
>
> Of course, there's no rule saying you have to back up only nightly. Since `repozo` and the sugary scripts we've wrapped it in are fast and don't do more I/O than necessary, it's not uncommon to do an incremental backup every hour or even every ten minutes. The advantage to more frequent backups is more choices for point-in-time restores. The disadvantage is hardly anything. For hourly backups, you can just move `back_up_zodb` into `/etc/cron.hourly`. For more frequent runs, you'll have to write your own crontab; again, see *Schedule manually*.

Tweak your filesystem backups

Of course, what ultimately gives you crash-proofness are your normal filesystem backups, which we assume are already in place. Here's what to include and exclude in those to ensure a smooth restoration of your Plone environment, should the worst happen:

- Back up the `/var/lib/plone/var/backup` directory, which contains all your full and incremental `Data.fs` backups.
- Do not back up `/var/lib/plone/var/filestorage/Data.fs`, as running backups while ZEO is up can yield an inconsistent copy.
- Optionally, exclude `/var/lib/plone/var/filestorage/Data.fs.old` to save space. You'll always get a consistent copy of this, though, so you might consider including it as one more safety net.
- Make sure to exclude `Data.fs.index`, `Data.fs.lock`, and `Data.fs.temp` from backups, as they'll cause nothing but heartache for you on restore. For example, if `Data.fs.index` somehow gets desynchronized with `Data.fs`, data corruption can result. More generally, whenever moving `Data.fs` files around, remember this simple rule about `Data.fs.index`: when in doubt, throw it out. It will be recreated automatically as soon as the database is used again.

What if I am a major credit card company?

If you can never, under any circumstances, stand to lose a single transaction or suffer a minute of downtime, there are a few good ways to do live replication and failover in ZODB. One good thing to research is RelStorage, which, instead of a `Data.fs` file, stores your data in a relational database. You can then use that database's replication facilities to ensure that no transactions are ever dropped. Another product that gives you the above plus ZEO failover is zeoraid. Instead of having one ZEO server as a single point of failure, you tell each Zope instance about several and can happily keep serving unless all of them fail simultaneously.

- Read more about RelStorage at `http://pypi.python.org/pypi/RelStorage`.
- zeoraid's documentation is at `http://pypi.python.org/pypi/gocept.zeoraid`.

Restore from backups

The previous preparation all pays off when you can recover from disaster fast and without thinking. Here is how to respond in the two most common restore scenarios: rebuilding after a nuclear attack and delving into the past to resurrect long-deleted content.

The smoking hole scenario

The worst has happened, and there's a smoking hole in the ground where your production server used to be. After replacing the floor panels, unboxing your new server, and restoring your filesystem-level backups onto it, it's time to restore the ZODB. This is breathtakingly simple:

1. Go into your buildout folder:
   ```
   cd /var/lib/plone
   ```
2. Delete your `Data.fs`, and make sure there is no `Data.fs` detritus lying around, lest you end up with an index file that doesn't match up with the database or a lockfile that keeps ZEO from starting:
   ```
   rm var/filestorage/Data.fs*
   ```
3. Restore from your incremental backups:
   ```
   bin/restore
   ```

That's it. `bin/restore` will copy over your most recent backup from the `/var/lib/plone/var/backup` directory. Fire up ZEO and your Zope instances, and be on your way.

The deletion disaster

The other common scenario is someone deleting something important from the Plone site but not realizing it until a week later, when our 7-day pack cycle has put it beyond reach of the ZMI's undo function. Meanwhile, many other changes have happened to the site, making a wholesale rollback to an earlier version impractical. In this situation...

1. Restore your buildout folder onto a spare machine.
2. Change directories into it.
   ```
   cd ~wherever/plone
   ```
3. Restore the ZODB to a point in time where the missing data still existed—in this example, January 29, 2010 at 1:03:05 p.m.:
   ```
   bin/restore 2010-01-29-13-03-05
   ```

Note that the time is in UTC, not the local time zone.

4. Start up ZEO and Zope on this spare machine, and either copy and paste the content (if there's not much of it), or use the ZMI's export and import functions to transfer it back to the production machine. Tedious? Absolutely. But it can make a lot of people very happy.

Upgrade add-on products

Few open source packages can be upgraded sanely without a serious dose of buyer-beware. Plone products, as mentioned in a previous chapter, are "free as in puppies", and one of the biggest opportunities for those puppies to make a mess comes during upgrades. Here's how to protect yourself so your data stays safe and your service reliable.

Performing product upgrades should be as simple as running `bin/buildout` to download and install the latest versions—and this often does work. However, buildout also makes a lot of assumptions that can lead to surprises:

- A stock Plone install relies on no fewer than three separate servers being up, and they do indeed go down from time to time, often without prior notice.
- The release of any product depends on the uncontested quality assertions of its developers—and the developers of any packages it depends on. The amount of testing done before uploading to PyPI (one major source of packages) or plone.org's Products section varies widely. Many buildout configurations will even download an alpha or beta version from PyPI in preference to a mature release.
- Even good practices like version pinning—a way to tell buildout to install certain versions of packages that you yourself have vetted—are unreliable: developers occasionally change packages without changing their version numbers, and PyPI does nothing to prevent this.

Thus, upgrading a product safely on a production server is a multi-step process:

1. Download a copy of the production buildout folder to a staging machine. This machine should be as similar to the production one as possible, in particular having Python at the same path. To save time, don't transfer the `Data.fs` files, as we'll replace them momentarily.

2. Move the downloaded buildout to the same path where it exists on the production server. Buildout tends to hard-code a lot of pathnames into the scripts it generates.
3. Use `bin/snapshotbackup` to get a consistent snapshot of the production `Data.fs`. Download it to the staging machine (virtual machines are handy for this) and put it in place in `var/filestorage`, throwing away any `Data.fs*` files that might already be there.
4. Edit `buildout.cfg` (if necessary) to bring in the upgraded product.
5. If you are using any egg or download caches outside the buildout folder, disable them. You may need to examine and edit the `.buildout/default.cfg` file in your home directory temporarily, for example. This causes any needed software to download into the buildout folder itself, making the environment self-contained.
6. Run `bin/buildout`.

If the buildout failed, chances are it's a transient error due to someone's release management mistake or a server outage. Asking whether anyone else is having similar errors on the `#plone` IRC channel on `irc.freenode.net` (or through the web interface at `http://plone.org/support/chat`) is a good first step toward diagnosing your problem.

If all went well, congratulations! Start up ZEO and Zope on your staging machine, and try out the new version of the product against your production data to make sure there are no unpleasant surprises:

- Try installing and uninstalling the product. Make sure uninstalling doesn't break the site.
- If the product provides content types, view, edit, and make new objects of those types, examining Zope's `event.log` or the output of `bin/instance fg` all the while.

Once you are satisfied with the new product, you can move your setup to the production server. It's often claimed that copying a `buildout.cfg` file and running `buildout` can reliably replicate a setup. However, because of the elements of unpredictability cited above, this is actually a fairly frightening way to upgrade a live server. A more reliable way is to move your staging environment, minus the disposable `Data.fs` you've been testing with, to your production server and then swap in the live `Data.fs`:

1. Shut down Zope and ZEO, and delete the `Data.fs` and any other `Data.fs.*` files from the `var/filestorage` folder of your staging buildout.

2. Copy the staging buildout folder to your production machine in an out-of-the-way spot.
3. Shut down ZEO and Zope on your production server.
4. Rename the production buildout, and move and rename the staging buildout (which is about to become your new production buildout) into the place of the old one.
5. Move the `Data.fs` from the old production buildout's `var/filestorage` folder into the new one.
6. Fire up the new buildout's ZEO and Zope, and all should be well!

Upgrade Plone

The precautions necessary when upgrading Plone itself are similar to those used when upgrading products. An overview of Plone's release process and history can also be informative when contemplating an upgrade:

- Plone's general version-numbering philosophy has been inconsistent over the life of the project, but it is currently as follows: a major release, such as 3.0 or 4.0, may unapologetically break backward compatibility with some third-party products, though migration paths for content (at least out-of-the-box sorts like news items and pages) are always included. Tenths- and hundredths-place releases (like 3.2 or 3.2.1, respectively), are mostly backward compatible with regard to add-ons. However, the complexity of the system and the lack of formal guidelines on what add-ons may and may not touch make backward compatibility less than one hundred percent. There are always some add-ons that break in a tenths-place release and a few unlucky ones for each hundredths-place release. As always, testing is crucial.
- Each major Plone release line, like the 3.x or 4.x series, has a different person in charge—the only people who are actually paid by the Plone Foundation. Though they usually stick to the above version numbering conventions, each release manager has a different ideal for the balance between backward compatibility and infrastructural advancement. Keep in mind that social as well as technical change often follows a new major release.
- With hundreds of third-party products—themselves of varying quality—the Plone team can't test against them all. And remember, no one else has exactly your data, either; Plone's extensive use of object persistence means that testing on one site doesn't necessarily predict what will happen on another. The importance of testing against production snapshots is thus not to be underestimated.

The recurring theme here is that you have to do your own quality assurance. Don't rush to upgrade to the latest Plone the week—or even the month—it comes out. Hang back, listen for problems on the `plone-users` and `plone-developers` mailing lists and on the `#plone` IRC channel, and test thoroughly against snapshots of your production data. When the time finally does come to upgrade, take careful backups as described in the *Upgrade add-on products* section earlier, and consult the upgrade instructions that come with the new release, since procedural details do change from time to time. With prudence and preparation, you can have a trouble-free Plone experience.

Summary

In this chapter, we've covered all the routine maintenance tasks you need to keep your Plone site happily zipping along:

- Packing the ZODB
- Backing up Plone, including incremental backups of the ZODB
- Upgrading add-on products without risking buildout going awry on a production server
- Upgrading Plone itself in a safe and controlled way

Index

A

B

C

Q

R

S

Thank you for buying
Plone 3 for Education

Packt Open Source Project Royalties

When we sell a book written on an Open Source project, we pay a royalty directly to that project. Therefore by purchasing Plone 3 for Education, Packt will have given some of the money received to the Plone project.

In the long term, we see ourselves and you—customers and readers of our books—as part of the Open Source ecosystem, providing sustainable revenue for the projects we publish on. Our aim at Packt is to establish publishing royalties as an essential part of the service and support a business model that sustains Open Source.

If you're working with an Open Source project that you would like us to publish on, and subsequently pay royalties to, please get in touch with us.

Writing for Packt

We welcome all inquiries from people who are interested in authoring. Book proposals should be sent to `author@packtpub.com`. If your book idea is still at an early stage and you would like to discuss it first before writing a formal book proposal, contact us; one of our commissioning editors will get in touch with you.

We're not just looking for published authors; if you have strong technical skills but no writing experience, our experienced editors can help you develop a writing career, or simply get some additional reward for your expertise.

About Packt Publishing

Packt, pronounced 'packed', published its first book "Mastering phpMyAdmin for Effective MySQL Management" in April 2004 and subsequently continued to specialize in publishing highly focused books on specific technologies and solutions.

Our books and publications share the experiences of your fellow IT professionals in adapting and customizing today's systems, applications, and frameworks. Our solution-based books give you the knowledge and power to customize the software and technologies you're using to get the job done. Packt books are more specific and less general than the IT books you have seen in the past. Our unique business model allows us to bring you more focused information, giving you more of what you need to know, and less of what you don't.

Packt is a modern, yet unique publishing company, which focuses on producing quality, cutting-edge books for communities of developers, administrators, and newbies alike. For more information, please visit our website: `www.PacktPub.com`.

Lightning Source UK Ltd.
Milton Keynes UK
27 December 2009

147933UK00002B/7/P

9 781847 198129